Browne Academy Curriculum

Kevin J. Browne

Table of Contents

For Teagan

"Non scholae sed vitae discimus."

Introduction

As an educator I have always wanted to write a book recommending the important books that everyone should read. Now, as a father I am focusing on educating my child and this project has assumed even greater importance. My belief, based on a fair amount of research on education is that the best education for a child involves the following components:

1. Active engagement with adults (parents in particular)
2. Hands-on tactile learning (let them explore, play, and touch)
3. Audio input (talk to your child, read to them, play music for them)
4. Reading (not textbooks but real books, good books, classics)

This curriculum is designed to foster these four components. To use the books in this curriculum and stress their importance to your child you need to read them yourself! Reading them as a family promotes discussing them as a family which is the kind of active engagement in learning that will keep your child interested in learning and make them a successful learner.

The recommended books are organized into "classes" but I use this term rather loosely. I think children should be encouraged to be curious and pursue those interests where they lead but as the guide for your child's learning your job is to provide the context for their current and future learning. That is what these classes do. It is also a way to provide an organized framework for assessing your child's progress.

To formalize the process of working through these classes I have developed a set of guidelines for completing a course. A certain number of books should be read and while this is flexible you should work to provide your child with a good dose of the basics in two categories of reading: the current literature in a field and the classics.

Each course contains separate lists for each of these with the current reading listed first and the classics listed second. You can customize the completion of each course as you like but you should not consider a course to be complete without reading at least some of the classics in that field.

There may be some objections to the structure of the courses in this curriculum. There are two important criticisms I want to answer. First, these books may be too difficult for young readers. While this may be true for some of the books a large proportion in every class are perfectly accessible to young readers. Those that are slightly more difficult can be postponed. However, the vast majority of works in this curriculum (even the classics) are within your grasp with some effort. But, this effort is an important part of the educational process. Learning takes work and while it can be fun, this lesson should be made clear to everyone.

A second criticism is that these courses leave off important material or books that ought to be read. However, one can make this argument regardless of the list for any course. Some limits have to be set and this means some books will be excluded. A major factor in inclusion here is the amount of impact a given work has had and the amount of connections that it allows a student to make between one subject and another. The bottom line though is that no approach which includes a list of books one ought to read will be perfect. You should feel free to add or subtract from these course lists. If you and your child are reading books and actively engaging in learning that is what counts. If my lists seem suspect, consult other lists. One thing you will find on almost all such recommended lists is a good dose of the classics. Virtually everyone agrees on these and for this reason the classics might be the best place to begin. Enjoy your learning as a family!

How to Use This Volume

Most people interested in a resource like this will probably already have ideas about how to use this volume. I have intentionally left out items often included in school curricula such as specific lesson plans, test resources, and specific assigned readings. There are many ways that these can be created using the books I've listed in the courses. I will describe my own plan for how to use this volume with my own family in the hopes that it will inspire ideas for you as well.

There are two main ways that this set of courses can be used. The first is a non-directed "unschooling" approach where parents let their children decide what subject they will learn and then use the book list for that course as a guide to begin gathering resources. For this approach many of the readings will easily lend themselves to assignments, experiments, field trips and other activities to assess learning. Parents who are already familiar with unschooling will be able to sue this as a supplemental resource to enhance their library.

A second approach using this volume is more directed. Here parents can use the organization I have laid out to emphasize mastery of certain core curriculum subjects such as those outlined in the moral and natural philosophy sections. For this approach I suggest laying out with your child specific goals for each course they decide to take such as the number of books to be read and what activities or assignments will be required to complete the course. One can also use the outline provided here to distinguish core courses from electives. The courses in the Other category provide a wide range of elective courses which can supplement the core courses and quite often connect to them and provide more specific and practical knowledge.

My strategy involves combining these approaches to provide some guidance while leaving the child free to explore different subjects and approaches to learning.

For each course I think it is important that mastery of the material be assessed using methods which require real world application of the material and not simply rote memorization and standard exams. When possible the material in the course should be connected with activities the entire family can engage in and learn from. The essays I have included on the importance of learning each major subject in the curriculum illustrate specific values that each course emphasizes and these can be used as the basis for application and assessment of course material.

Concretely, students should be expected to be able to talk and write about each subject they are studying. The should also be expected to connect subjects they are learning to material they have previously learned. This curriculum is not about passing courses and then forgetting the knowledge acquired.

An important component in this approach to education is making connections. This may come slowly at first but as the philosopher Ludwig Wittgenstein once said "Light dawns gradually over the whole." The more you delve into the material here and the more you learn about each subject the easier it will be to make connections. This is where the fun of learning really begins!

What do we want students to learn?

This has become an important question for me as the father of an almost 2 year old child. The world of education is filled with theories on what children need to learn and how best to teach them. I think we can safely say that we want our children to end up happy, healthy, well-adjusted, self-actualized, self-sufficient, contributing members of the human community. The question is how do we help them achieve these ends? In current terminology, what are our learning outcomes?

I actually dislike the "learning outcomes approach" in general because, among other things, it presumes that we can push the right buttons in our students and they will automatically respond. But, in reality learning is each individual's own responsibility and what educators can do best is set the stage and create supportive conditions for children to have the best chance of learning and succeeding in their education. Ideally, educators should be mentors.

But, even though there are problems with the outcomes approach to education, it does make sense to ask what some general goals should be for educating our children, whatever model we choose to foster these goals. I think some of the most important goals are as follows (I've placed the specific subjects from my curriculum in parentheses that seem to support the specified goal):

Creativity: The ability to be creative, in both one's personal as well as professional life, is an important skill and one that too often seems to be educated out of children. To foster this skill it is important to expose children to many different forms of art as well different ways of thinking about things in general. This is one of those skills that can be easily incorporated into almost any subject but it can also too easily be overlooked in an effort to teach a specific subject in a specific orthodox way. (Art, Poetry, Plays, Thinking)

Problem Solving: One of the main reasons to foster creativity is to help improve problem-solving skills. This is a component that can also be easily integrated into almost any subject as an active part of learning. The emphasis here is on the application and use of knowledge as opposed to the mere acquisition of knowledge. (Math, Thinking)

Life Skills: By the term "life skills" I mean several different things. Certainly this would include such areas as finance (i.e. saving/investing/debt management), time management, and cooking but it should also include interpersonal skills as well to foster the ability to get along with others, form lasting friendships, romantic relationships, and work related skills. (Life Skills)

Literacy: This obviously involves the first two of the 3 R's: Reading and Writing. But I think literacy also involves good communication skills in general and so should include public speaking. Also, to be included in this broad area is cultural literacy and a familiarity with literature and language. (Language, Reading and Writing)

Numeracy: The third of the 3 R's: Mathematics. But, numeracy entails something besides knowing the basics of algebra, geometry and calculus. More importantly it involves having a good sense of numbers, being able to understand and use statistics, and having a good handle on practical everyday math. (Mathematics, Thinking)

Self-Learning: Ideally, learning is not something that stops once a child finishes school and graduates. Learning is a life-long process and one that is largely in the hands of each individual. The best we can offer to our children is a set of good learning skills such as those mentioned above and a broad exposure to the basics of human knowledge. Along with this we should cultivate in them the ability to learn on their own since we cannot hope to teach them everything they will ever need to know in their lifetime. We can get them started and encourage them to keep learning but where they end up and what they need to know to get their is to some extent out of our hands.

Having said that, I think the case can be made that there are some specific subjects that ought to be taught as a way of fostering these general skills and broadening our children's horizons.

The Utility of Learning

Before I begin the series of essays on the importance of learning various subjects in common course curricula, I thought it might be useful to pause a moment to ponder on the connection between utility and learning. The question "When am I ever going to use this?" is the bane of every teacher's existence. What it implies is that the only things worth learning are those that will be used. I will be arguing in the forthcoming series that you can make a utility related argument for each and every major subject in the curriculum but what if you couldn't make such an argument? What if a particular subject such as history or music or philosophy had no use? Is it no longer worth learning?

There are several problems with using utility as the sole criterion to determine what ought to be taught and what ought to be learned. First, there are other good reasons to learn most anything. Second, there is really no way to predict what specific subject or part of a subject will be useful to someone in the future with any accuracy.

Why should we only be interested in learning things that are useful? As the physicist Richard Feynman noted, a sufficient reason for learning is simply "the pleasure of finding things out." So what if you don't use what you've just learned? It is simply inherently enjoyable to learn new things; or it should be. While not everyone will enjoy learning the same things, if you find no joy in learning something new independent of whether you will use the knowledge this is not a problem with the subject matter itself but may be a problem with your attitude towards learning. By emphasizing utility we have trained students to only value that which has immediate and obvious utility and this is a mistake since it deprives them of this joy of learning.

To say that the only things worth learning are those with utility implies that we can know with certainty what will be useful. While this may be true in the short-term, it becomes more difficult to judge the utility of a subject the farther ahead and more long-term we look. As another physicist, Niels Bohr, once said "prediction is difficult especially about the future." We really can't know what specific subjects or parts of subjects will be useful in the future. If we only teach what seems practical and useful in the present we are surely robbing ourselves of useful insights and learning that will serve us well in the future.

But, I can hear the criticism from some already. There are some subjects that have never been useful to anyone. Some things are just pointless to learn. I hesitate to list what some of these subjects might be but perhaps you already have one or two in mind. If so, I invite you to join me as I try to lay out the case for every major subject being important to learn. I will be focusing mostly on utility but I hope to have shown here that there is no reason to concede the argument for learning something just because it has no obvious or immediate utility.

The Importance of Art

We begin this series of articles on the importance of learning the various academic subjects with art. From there I'll be proceeding alphabetically through the curriculum. Art is often the first subject to be cut when budget constraints loom and this is likely because it seems less central to learning. After all, what practical values are served by learning art?

As I tell students in my introduction to logic course, many subjects have an indirect value to education. That is, while learning the subject matter may not seem practical, the act of learning itself is valuable. For most courses though it is possible to determine direct and indirect values so let's look at art in this light.

By art I mean the visual, plastic arts such as painting and sculpture. The importance of learning about these arts is not only in studying past works but in practicing art as well. Why could learning about these arts be valuable? There are several benefits including improving one's skills in abstraction, imagination, and creativity.

Abstraction: For much art, even representational art, learning to appreciate it encourages the ability to reason in the abstract. Since art involves the use of symbols to convey concepts

Imagination: Another benefit of studying art is to improve one's imagination. While studying past works of art helps improve one's ability to reason in the abstract, practicing art helps fire the imagination.

Creativity: Related to this is the benefit of improving one's creativity. One of the central values of any education is fostering creativity. Not only is this a vital skill in your work life but it is also one of life's important values.

Finally, I should mention the fact that art provides an important means of understanding and appreciating beauty. But, still, one can ask about the practical value of improving one's abstraction, imagination, and creativity. Art allows us the opportunity to see the world in new ways with minimal risk. We can try out new options, new perspectives, and new ways of approaching life and its problems in a risk free space. As Morse Peckham points out in his book *Man's Rage For Chaos: Biology, Behavior, and the Arts*, "art is a rehearsal for the orientation that makes innovation possible." In a world driven by information and innovation, what could be more practical?

The Importance of Astronomy

At some time nearly everyone looks up in the sky in wonder. There are so many stars, galaxies, and empty space. Are we alone? Could there be other planets which are teeming with life as Earth is? Did everything really begin with a Big Bang? So many questions but they seem to have no answers. Are there benefits to studying astronomy even if such questions cannot be answered? Let's look at it.

Questions such as the ones listed above should seem important in and of themselves whether or not the answers are easily found or whether the answers have any practical significance. The study of such questions seems to be a deeply human exercise and one worth the time and effort.

Perspective: Sometimes our problems seem so immense and, our accomplishments so outstanding, our importance as humans a given. But, contemplating the universe and its origins can help to put our own lives into perspective. We needn't feel any less proud of what we've accomplished or feel that our lives have less meaning in the face of such contemplation. However, sometimes it is useful to contemplate something larger than ourselves and consider how we fit into it. What could be a more appropriate subject of such contemplation as the universe?

Orientation: Closely related to perspective, knowing where you are and how you relate to others is of fundamental importance (and an important aspect of learning geography which I will address in a later post). Certainly orienting yourself in the larger context of the solar system, galaxy, and universe completes this process.

Understanding: Our attempts to discover the origin of the universe have also contributed to our understanding of the fundamental nature of reality which is, at least partly, explained by two major scientific theories: relativity and quantum mechanics. Each of these theories provides surprising, and surprisingly useful, insights into how the world we inhabit works.

Exploration: A fundamental human drive to explore can be satisfied, if only indirectly, by studying the soar system, or own galaxy, and the universe as a whole.

The very rhythm of our days, months, and years is set by what happens in the world that astronomy explores. Recognizing this and understanding it fulfills fundamental our human need to explore, understand, and satisfy curiosity. Observing the movements of the moon and stars puts us in touch with something larger than ourselves, forces us to re-orient our perspective and sense of time, and in a busy, hurried, stressful world in which we live, such values are important to remember and cultivate in a way that studying astronomy uniquely facilitates.

The Importance of Biology

It would seem fairly obvious that biology is important. As the study of life, an understanding of biology is critical to many areas of our lives including our health and well-being. In addition to this, understanding biology allows us to appreciate what Richard Dawkins calls "the greatest show on Earth:" evolution. In addition to some standard reasons for studying biology I want to examine some other values that biology helps to foster.'

Health: A common argument for studying biology is that it helps us understand how to improve our health and diet. No doubt this is a good reason and the most practical one to examine. What could be more important as a basis for living a good life that to be reasonably healthy?

Interdependence: Life on Earth is interdependent in many different ways from predator and prey to symbiosis. Studying biology places us firmly into this interdependent web of life.

Ingenuity: The demands of survival in the wild lead to some pretty ingenious habits in plants and animals. Not only are these amazing and interesting to learn about but can potentially provide inspiration for human problem solving as well.

Endurance: Life thrives in the most unlikely places from deep in the ocean, hidden in dark caves, freezing and near boiling water. All demonstrate the endurance of life. As the Jeff Goldblum character in Jurassic Park said, "life finds a way." Again, not only in this immensely interesting to learn about, it can be inspirational as well. No matter how difficult our lives seem and how insurmountable our problems appear, there is always a way to endure and prevail.

Evolution: One of the most important, not to mention well tested and observed theories in science is the theory of evolution by natural selection. Understanding this theory is a major step in anyone's education as it is often counter intuitive and not immediately obvious or easily observable on the short time span of a human life. But, understanding it ought to be a major goal of the study of biology and is a rewarding pursuit. As Darwin recognized, "There is grandeur in this view of life." What better argument for studying biology than the appreciation of such grandeur and an understanding of our place in it.

The Importance of Chemistry

I remember as a kid being very bored in chemistry class. A few experiments here and there and a mountain of equations somehow could not compel me to curiosity for molecules and chemical reactions. How unfortunate. Chemistry is not only fascinating to study and practice but important as well. It is a window into the foundations of biology and physics and can provide insights both practical and interesting.

Foundations: At the core of both biology and physics is chemistry since this science addresses how molecules interact and connect with each other. Any understanding of how things work in the world, both organic and inorganic eventually comes down to chemistry. Of course, this begs the question, why should anyone care about understanding how things work in the world at all.

Health: One reason to care about understanding is that it is good for our health. What we eat, how it is cooked, and how it is digested are all functions of chemistry and understanding the chemistry involved is an important step towards taking charge of one's own health.

Connections: Chemistry is about how molecules connect and interact but can chemistry give us any insight into our human and social connections? Perhaps. Often in chemical reactions the result is much different in composition than the original inputs. Dangerous elements can mix to create beneficial molecules; salt is a good example of this. Unexpected results are a part of connections in life as well. Benefits come from such connections all of the time.

There are so many practical benefits to the study of

chemistry it is hard to provide a broad overview in such a short space. But, if you think about it nearly every part of your life is related in some way to chemistry. What you wear, eat, drive, where you live, the air you breathe, what medicines you take. All of these areas of your life where you have to make decisions would be enhanced by some working knowledge of chemistry. So, take a look around and see how your life is touched by chemistry and begin to study these areas on a molecular level. You never know what you might learn and what connections you might make!

The Importance of Economics

Surely one of the easier subjects to show the importance of is economics. Yet, while it has obvious practical benefits it seems to be rarely taught well or with an eye towards understanding fundamental principles or how they apply in the real world. Economics courses seem to be heavily skewed towards explaining theory but not practice. That is, when such courses are taught at all. Often this is not the case in primary and secondary schools. No wonder people's money management skills are often so poor.

Money Management: Of course, this is the main practical benefit of learning about economics. While the study of economics, in and of itself, will not make you wealthy, failing to learn and apply basic principles of saving and investing will surely keep you poor. Millions of people were raised to believe, and many still do believe, that investing is nothing more than gambling and no more reliable as a way to build wealth and financial security than buying lottery tickets. Still more believe that credit cards represent free money and have already spent their next raise without ever seeing the money. The study of economics is a good first step towards fixing some of these problems both in one's personal life and in our nation which also suffers from poor economic thinking and planning.

Value: The notion of value is important both in economics and life in general. Thomas Sowell points out that many people wrongly criticize economics by pointing out that there are also such things as "non-economic values," to which he responds by saying that of course there are non-economic values. In fact, there are only non-economic values. Economics is not a value itself but a way of determining the costs and benefits of trading one value for another.

Trade-Offs: The notion of trade-offs is a difficult one for many to accept. In a complex world we often want simple solutions but sometimes there are no solutions at all, only trade-offs. We can spend more money on groceries only if we are willing to spend less on shoes. We drive safer by slowing down only if we are willing to spend more time on the road. Many areas of life involve such trade-offs and economics provides a clear method for thinking through how to make these trade-offs in the best way possible.

Planning: In *Basic Economics*, Thomas Sowell writes about his experience as an undergraduate in economics: "When I was an undergraduate studying economics under Professor Arthur Smithies of Harvard, he asked me in class one day what policy I favored on a particular issue of the times. Since I had strong feelings on that issue, I proceeded to answer him with enthusiasm, explaining what beneficial consequences I expected from the policy I advocated.

"And then what will happen" he asked.

The question caught me off guard. However, as I thought about it, it became clear that the situation I described would lead to other economic consequences, which I then began to consider and to spell out.

"And then what will happen after that?" Professor Smithies asked."

This continued for several more rounds until: "By now I was beginning to see that the economic reverberations of the policy I advocated were likely to be pretty disastrous and in fact, much worse than the initial situation that it was designed to improve."

The world is filled with such examples of the failure to think things through beyond the first stage. As the economist Bastiat pointed out, good economists see beyond the visible consequences of their actions to the less visible and unintended consequences. While not immediately visible itself, this is one of the most important benefits of the study of economics.

The Importance of Ethics

The more I teach courses in ethics the more convinced I become that people are not being taught basic ethical principles at all; either in the home or at school. I say this not because people are behaving more unethically than ever before (although there is much of that going on) but because of how my students talk about ethics. They seem genuinely confused about what should be some very basic principles in ethics which, if taught, could have a positive impact.

The case for teaching ethics really comes down to what Aristotle said. The person who acts virtuously is simply happier in their life. Recent studies in psychology bear this out. People who lie, cheat, and steal are rarely if ever happy and people who are happy do not seem as tempted to lie, cheat, and steal. Aside from being happier here are a few other benefits to the study of ethics.

Empathy: A core principle in nearly every ethical theory taught in philosophy and nearly every moral code in human cultures is empathy. Having a genuine concern for others and being able to put yourself in their shoes is not only an important ethical principle but a useful life skill.

Virtue: This concept seems outdated but is an important part of most moral codes even if it is called something else. The basic idea here is that there are a core set of principles that it is good for one to have and act on such as honesty, friendship, contemplation. The last two were among the most important for Aristotle and though not often thought of as ethical principles are important to a happy life. The point comes back to the one made above. Why should one know about ethics and act according to ethical principles? Because it leads to a happier life.

The study of ethics can also help answer some very basic but important questions about how the world works and that ethics has an objective and universal component:

What makes an action right or wrong?

Who decides what is right and wrong?

Does everyone have different morals?

There is much that we now know thanks to the study of evolutionary psychology about the answers to these questions. This information is quite interesting and useful. Ethics is something that should be taught starting at a young age but parents who are ill informed about the basic principles of ethics will have a harder time passing on useful knowledge to their children and providing answers to these important questions. If for no other reason than to benefit your children the study of ethics should be seen as an important priority in your education.

The Importance of Geology & Geography

For many people the study of geology is just about looking at rocks and the study of geography is nothing more than memorizing state capitals to be forgotten later on. While it is useful to be able to remember capitals and interesting to identify rocks, there are other reasons to study geology and geography.

We live in a world where information travels at the speed of light and what happens on the other side of the globe (both natural and political) effects us. And we all know the statistics regarding the poor knowledge young people have related to geography:

-Only 37% of young Americans can find Iraq on a map—though U.S. troops have been there since 2003.
-6 in 10 young Americans don't speak a foreign language fluently.
-20% of young Americans think Sudan is in Asia. (It's the largest country in Africa.)
-48% of young Americans believe the majority population in India is Muslim. (It's Hindu—by a landslide.)
-Half of young Americans can't find New York on a map.

This ignorance has profoundly negative consequences. But, I want to argue that there are bigger reasons for studying these sciences.

Perspective: Taking a wider perspective can be very useful and the study of geography encourages us to do this with regard to space. The study of geology reminds us to have perspective with regard to time. We often think that what happens in our little corner of the world at a particular time is all-important but the world is much larger and time much longer than the framework in which we ordinarily conceive of things. Adopting a larger view of time and space can be useful.

Orientation: We need to orient ourselves both literally and figuratively in the world in which we live. As Jared Diamond points out in his book *Guns, Germs, and Steel,* much of our history turns on the contingencies of geology and geography. We inhabit a world of forces much larger than ourselves and these have a profound effect on our life and well-being. Thus, some understanding of these forces helps us to appreciate our history and out future.

Incremental Change: Throughout geological history, profound changes have occurred by the slow and deliberate processes of nature. Simple wind and water erosion formed the Grand Canyon. What can we learn from this? The power of small steps, consistently taken, yields large effects. This is abundantly true and nature and in our own lives. Slow and steady winds the race.

Personally, it took me some time to warm up to the study of geology. My sister was an avid amateur geologist and tried to spark the passion in me but it did not take hold until much later and even then in much weaker form. But, I hope to rectify that with my daughter and teach her to appreciate the natural world by instilling in her an understanding of the powerful processes at work in the natural world.

Knowing where you are going is not possible unless you know where you are and where you came from,. This is true of history which I will discuss in my next post but equally true of the sciences of geology and geography. For that reason, their study should be a part of any good education.

The Importance of History

On the 50th anniversary of D-Day I wrote an essay titled "IS D-Day Worth Remembering?" My hope was to provide an argument for the importance of learning history sufficiently motivating to cause students to act on it. I'm not sure I succeeded. But, the question is still valid to ask about any event of historical significance. If you feel some discomfort at the question this is likely because you recognize that the answer is yes, such events are worth remembering and it's unfortunate to have to provide an argument for this. If you don't think such historical events are worth remembering, please read on for more reasons to study history.

Orientation: As I noted in the essay on geology and geography, if you don't know where you are, you don't know where you're going. This is true of history as well. If you don't know where you came from, you can't know where you're going. History provides the context for where we each start our journey in life. Others have come before us and have literally set the stage for us. Failing to understand this impedes our ability to fully engage in life.

Experience: As Sir Isaac Newton once said "if I have seen further than most it is because I have stood on the shoulders of giants." This perfectly captures the importance of studying history no matter what you're interests are. Every field of study and ever human occupation has a history and has its giants. You can benefit from their experience and learn from their mistakes. You don't have to reinvent the wheel. Others have done it and it is easy to forget this without studying the past. We can literally benefit from the experience of those who came before us, even as we benefit from the experience of those who have been on the job longer than us at work. They know the ropes because they were there before us. History is nothing more than the study of those who were there before us and know the ropes.

Commonality: We tend to think that people in the past were very different from us and superficially this is true. This is what causes some to dismiss the argument made above from experience. Those who lived in the past had different technology, different housing, they ate different food, wore different clothes. But, in the areas of life that really count, there is a strong bond of commonality which transcends time. People in the past had the same concerns about life, the same emotions of love and hate, the same ultimate questions and problems. Their solutions often differed but we can learn something of value by understanding their similarities as well as their differences.

Drama: To students who say history is boring I ask: Is life today boring? If you answer no, then remember this. What students in the future will study as history is your life today. What would you say to them if they said that their history was boring? In truth, history is the study of the drama of human life and that drama is no less interesting for having happened in the past than it is now. If you think history is boring this means you have not really been studying history but rather a school textbook version of history which bears little resemblance to the real thing.

Remembering: Finally, I want to argue that the act of remembering in and of itself is a sufficient reason to study history. If you have a relative who fought in a war, helped others in some way in their work, created something artistic, devoted themselves to public service, or was simply a good role model to their family, isn't this person worth remembering? Don't we dishonor them by not remembering? But, in a larger sense, everyone fits into one of the categories above. In a practical sense, we cannot truly remember every single person who has come before us. But, history provides us a way of remembering even those whose names we no longer know. D-Day is worth remembering because it involved so many people just like you and me who made their contributions and lived their life without any thought of what future generations might think about them. They did their jobs, loved their families, made names for themselves (or not) and the very least we owe them is some act of remembering, even if this involves nothing more than the study of history.

The Importance of Language

What I want to argue for here is not the importance of learning language. That should be obvious. Learning to speak a language is a virtual inevitability given the proper amount of exposure to language early in a child's life. What I want to argue for is that it is important to push beyond elementary proficiency to advance one's skills not only in spoken language, through a continually expanding vocabulary, but also in written language through the proper use of grammar, spelling, and the ability to write well in various contexts.

The practical benefits of these skills should be obvious as well but sadly even with so many benefits, these skills are sorely lacking and not often taught at all. The fashionable idea that teaching children proper grammar and spelling is continuing to do vastly more harm than good. And, it flies in the face of historical reality. We know that authors and poets as great as Dickens, Shakespeare, and many others were steeped in the rules of proper grammar without stifling their creativity. Rules of expression, in language as in art, don't stifle creativity but provide a meaningful context within which it can occur. Additionally, you cannot break the rules if you've never been taught the rules in the first place!

Communication: An obvious benefit of language is communication. But, the real benefits of this are better realized once one advances beyond the rudimentary forms of language use. An expanded vocabulary and advanced writing ability enhance the ability to communicate. There are subtle concepts as well as complex ones that simply cannot be expressed with barely grammatical middle school level language skills.

Many of my students complain that the texts they are

required to read in college are too complex and difficult to understand. But, this is more a reflection on their poor skills than it is the complexity of the text. What these students are really experiencing is the penalty of their poor education in such areas as vocabulary and grammar. Again, subtle and complex concepts require subtle and complex language to convey. To understand them, the reader must have comparable skills.

Expression: To appreciate the aesthetics of language also requires advanced skills. Like communication, the benefit here is twofold. First, there is the benefit of appreciating literature, poetry, and even philosophy and history. Second, there is the benefit of being able to be expressive. Conveying the wide range of human emotions so important to a well-lived life requires the kind of skills learning language provides.

Abstraction: Lastly, the ability to think abstractly is greatly enhanced by advanced language skills. Granted these skills would be unimportant if one never had to deal with abstract concepts but our entire life is affected by such concepts. Love, freedom, truth, and beauty are just a few of such concepts which have major importance in our lives. To think of such concepts requires a language skill that goes beyond the concrete.

The ability to speak and write well is often seen as an indicator of underlying intelligence. Right or wrong, people will judge you by your language skills. For this reason as well as those listed above it is important to learn these skills early and practice them often.

The Importance of Literature

"Fictional characters behave according to the same psychological probabilities as real people. But the characters of fiction are found in exotic dilemmas that real people hardly encounter. Consequently, fiction provides us with the opportunity to ponder how people react in uncommon situations, and to deduce moral lessons, psychological principles, and philosophical insights from their behavior."
J.R. McCuen and A.C. Winkler

I first ran across this quote in an introductory logic textbook as an example of an argument. It is precisely the argument I want to advance here for the importance of studying literature. Like all art, literature in the form of novels, plays, and even poetry gives us a chance to rehearse scenarios and address ultimate life questions. We can work through moral dilemmas, grief, death, love, and other human emotions and dramas and find lessons to apply to everyday life.

Narrative: We often learn better by reading and telling stories than simply trying to learn facts out of context. This is why it is best to learn history as a narrative. Unfortunately, history textbooks do not read well as stories. With literature we have a ready-made vehicle to learn about the past in an entertaining and engaging way.

Ethics: One of the best ways to discuss ethics is to use real world examples and case studies. But, like history textbooks these can often be dry and not very engaging. They also force us to examine complex issues without appealing to the real world complexity and context of a given situation. Interestingly enough, good literature can provide this complexity and context even though the characters and situations described are not real. With this context, we can use literature to examine problems in ethics and possible solutions to moral dilemmas.

Problem Solving: In a more general sense, literature provides us with a vehicle for exercising problem solving skills. Even though fictional characters do end up in "exotic dilemmas," they are often not entirely dissimilar from our own dilemmas and though I am not arguing that we ought to do as fictional characters do, we can often learn something by the insights that can be gained in the study of literature. Even if we learn what not to do this can be a valuable lesson.

Role Models: Literature provides us with a wide array of characters to study and many of these can be used as good role models. Like real people, fictional characters (at least those in good literature) are often flawed but this allows us to explore the full complexity of humanity as we decide which role models to emulate and which to avoid. Even the best real life heroes have traits we ought to avoid.

Students often ask why they are required to study past works of fiction that seem irrelevant to their life today. But, the best works of literature are still read and studied precisely because they contain characters and lessons that are timeless. Reading only recent and obviously relevant works denies us the opportunity to learn from a wide range of sources and limits our scope to only what we can see immediately before us. But, the world is a much larger place, both geographically and historically. Literature provides an entertaining way to learn this lesson and can be a window onto many other important subjects in the curriculum. It can also show us how these subjects connect and influence life. With all of these benefits it is well worth studying the great works of literature.

The Importance of Mathematics

While it's relatively easy to argue for the importance of studying mathematics, it is unfortunate to have to. But, the fact remains that in some cases a majority of college students enter their freshman year needing some remedial mathematics courses. This clearly indicates that they are not getting a good math education in high school and probably also means they are not being shown the importance of learning math. This is more unfortunate as the job market continues to develop more and more jobs where math skills are in demand. Even in the information age, where information is usually taken to mean verbal or written communication, mathematics still ranks as an important skill set.

Everyday Use: The most obvious argument for studying math is the many everyday uses. Calculating percentages, balancing a checkbook, calculating area are just a few skills everyone needs virtually every day of their lives. Unfortunately, such applied math skills are sorely lacking even in students with good grades in high school math courses. The philosopher and mathematician Pythagoras recognized that numbers are an integral part of every life and that has never been more true than today.

Numeracy: One of the most important aspects of studying math is gaining what mathematician John Allen Paulos calls numeracy, defined as a general familiarity with numbers or having a good sense of numbers. This is quite different than being skilled in everyday uses of math though the two are connected. Being numerate involves such skills as estimation and a firm grasp of statistical principles and how to apply them. Being numerate also involves being able to see the connections between numbers and aspects of life not immediately obvious and not often taught in math classes. What does the population of a city tell you about how many ethnic restaurants there are or the chances of finding a good used bookstore?

Universality: In many areas of life people tend to be relativists in spite of the many problems with this view especially in the realm of ethics. But, the study of mathematics can be a good antidote to this relativism as it shows that there are certain universal principles which govern how the world works and how we can understand it which are independent of culture or opinion. There is no such thing as Chinese mathematics which differs from European mathematics. The same principles apply wherever you happen to live.

Foundations: Perhaps for reasons connected with the points made above about universal rules, Plato advised that before studying philosophy and ethics students in his Academy first master the principles of mathematics and geometry. Pythagoras believed that everything consisted of numbers and to the extent that we can quantify a wide range of phenomena both physical and social this is true. Mathematics is the foundation of physics, chemistry, and most other hard sciences. Through the use of statistics it can also be seen as an integral part of such soft sciences as sociology and economics. To fully understand the principles of these disciplines requires a good working knowledge of mathematics.

More than any other area in the curriculum, with the possible exception of history, how math is taught has led to the problem of mathematical illiteracy. Unless we begin teaching mathematics with an eye towards helping students to master everyday use and gain numeracy as well as see the connections and foundations of math in other disciplines we will continue to struggle in a world more driven by math than ever. Ultimately, students will grow into adults who see first-hand the costs of this illiteracy in their shrinking income, investments, and savings. Perhaps those numbers will motivate the drive towards improved math literacy!

The Importance of Music

Among the first subjects to be cut in school budgets are art and music. These cuts are often based on the belief that these subjects can be sacrificed without much damage to a student's development or academic success. But, more and more research shows that this is not the case. While the Mozart Effect, claiming an increase in IQ points when children are exposed to classical music, has been largely debunked, there are still good reasons to study music. Let's consider some of these.

Applied Academics: One benefit of the study of music is that it can show the fun application of other academic subjects such as mathematics, physics, history, and geography. Given the general interest in music that most children have, it can be used as a window into other subjects that are not as immediately interesting for students.

Cognitive Benefits: While the Mozart Effect may not be reliable, there are tangible cognitive developmental benefits to studying music. Surely one of these is an increase in creativity. Other benefits include an increase in attention span and quantitative ability. Music does activate various parts of the brain and this increased activity has positive benefits. Music rewards close attention to detail, form, structure, and organization all of which are beneficial in many other areas of life.

Rhythm: An important part of music is the element of rhythm and many children relate to music very physically though dance, clapping, singing, and humming. Focusing on the rhythm of music can improve a child's general physical coordination and practicing a musical instrument can improve more specific coordination and dexterity.

Harmony: A second component of music is harmony and here the benefits of studying music are both literal and metaphorical. The study of harmony develops the ability to hear and discriminate among various tones and intervals and can lead to an appreciation of a wider range of musical styles. Metaphorically the study of harmony can be used as a means of teaching the benefit of harmony in general in how we relate to others. Such virtues as sharing and cooperation can be introduced through the musical element of harmony.

Melody: Built on the foundation of rhythm and harmony is the element of melody. Again, the benefits of study here are both literal and metaphorical. Since music has long been used as an aid to memory and a means of improving memory, the study of melody can be beneficial. The study of increasingly complex melodies can lead to an improvement of memory for more complex ideas as well. Metaphorically, the study of melody introduces the idea of individuality. Like musical pieces, everyone has their own individual melody which develops over time.

Just a consideration of the basic elements of music can illustrate several important benefits to studying music. Studying specific genres can yield other benefits. Jazz is important to the study and ability of improvisation. The blues illustrates emotional expression. Classical music reveals organization and precision. At the same time, music also shows the universal nature of such values as every genre contains these elements as well as the basics of rhythm, harmony, and melody. The rewards of studying and enjoying music extend far beyond the simple act of listening and playing. As important as these are, the applied benefits are also well worth examining.

The Importance of Philosophy

For most people philosophy is an unfamiliar subject to begin with so to argue that it is useful in everyday life might seem like a difficult proposition. Yet, with the growth of applied philosophy and the practice of philosophical counseling, philosophy has taken on a new sense of importance. In truth, philosophy has always been important. As Epicurus pointed out "Vain is the word of a philosopher which does not heal any suffering. For just as there is no profit in medicine if it does not expel the diseases of the body, so there is no profit in philosophy either, if it does not expel the suffering of the mind."

Therapy for the Sane: Lou Marinoff has called the practice of philosophy "therapy for the sane." This is a good description of the recent philosophical counseling movement but as the Epicurus quote illustrates philosophers have always been concerned with improving life and relieving suffering. It is only recent movements such as analytic philosophy which have moved away from this tradition. Philosophy invites us to reflect on how we can lead a happy and meaningful life. It also provides an opportunity to address life's ultimate questions involving suffering and death and in the best sense of the word is, indeed therapy understood as care of the soul.

Power of Ideas: Philosophy is really about the study of ideas and their power in our lives. Alfred Adler once said "A person's behavior springs from his ideas." So, the study of ideas is important not only to understand the actions of others but ourselves. Our life is ultimately guided by many ideas such as truth, beauty, justice, meaning, and good to name just a few. A systematic study of these can lead to a greater understanding of some of the most important aspects of our life.

Meaning: The question for meaning is one of the most important aspects of anyone's life and the psychiatrist Viktor Frankl recognized that a large amount of psychological suffering results from the failure to find meaning. His approach to therapy called Logotherapy is premised on the idea that finding meaning is an important key to mental health. Philosophy provides a method for examining our life and the attempt to find meaning.

The study of philosophy is often seen as an abstract exercise with very little relevance to everyday life and the problems real people encounter. But, the best of philosophy provides just the kinds of insights one needs to address life's ultimate questions and help find meaning and purpose in life. Furthermore, we are influenced each and every day by a world of ideas. Studying them in an effort to understand them and their effect on us is a worthy and important pursuit.

The Importance of Physics

The scientist J.B.S. Haldane once said "My own suspicion is that the Universe is not only queerer than we suppose, but queerer than we can suppose." This is the daunting prospect facing anyone who tries to understand how the world works and where everything came from. But, this is precisely what physics attempts to do and with the advances made in relativity and quantum mechanics we have made progress. Yes, there are still unanswered questions but as strange as the implications of relativity and quantum mechanics are their accuracy so far tells us that they are good explanations as far as they go. But, the question remains. If the universe is "queerer than we can suppose," is there any point or benefit in studying the science that studies the universe? Let's look at some possible benefits.

Appearance/Reality: An important distinction made by early philosophers and scientists still holds true and is a useful one to remember in everyday life. There is a difference between appearance and reality. In other words, things are not always what they seem. Physical objects appear to be solid yet we know the reality is that they are composed of very tiny particles which themselves are in constant motion and which consist of largely empty space. Many of our common sense intuitions about how the world works are based on appearances and are wrong. We would do we to remember that to truly understand anything it is important to look below the surface to the reality underneath.

Wonder: The practical benefit of our everyday perspective allows us to get on with the business of living without having to deal with the realities that physics describes. As Richard Dawkins points out, we have evolved to live in a middle world between the immensely large objects in the universe such as galaxies and the vanishingly small objects in the world such as electrons and quarks. Our minds are not innately tuned to observe these levels or to comprehend them without great effort. But, as a result of being evolved to live in this middle world we can lose some of the sense of wonder that comes from a study of the large and the small. Physics helps us regain this important feeling of wonder.

Connections: Physics also shows that everything is ultimately connected in many surprising ways. If you contemplate how the universe of the large looks from the perspective of galaxies and groups of galaxies you quickly see that there is no way to distinguish individual people here on earth. Likewise, if you contemplate the universe of the small from the perspective of an electron or a quark you also recognize that there is no way to distinguish individuals. This shift in perspective from the everyday to the physics based perspective reveals a world more connected than we usually consider. Appreciating that is an important insight and one which has many uses in everyday life.

Of course, there are also many very tangibly practical benefits to studying physics in a world based on the flow of digital information and technology. None of this would be possible without the advances made in physics. While we may not contemplate the queerness of the universe on a daily basis we do live with the results of our knowledge of this queer universe. The power of these results will continue to grow over the next few decades and an understanding of the forces behind these advances in technology will be invaluable.

The Importance of Politics

At any given time in history it is relatively easy to find politicians who have fallen out of favor with the people they are charged with representing or leading. In the United States congressional disapproval seems higher than ever. Many people instinctively distrust politicians and many otherwise well qualified people are put off pursuing public service entirely once they observe what those who seek elected office must endure to win an election. Given all of this, can there be any good benefits to the study of politics? Since the essence of politics is the act of coming together in civil society to solve the problems in that society it seems that there certainly practical benefits to the study of this much maligned subject.

Cooperation: An important element of politics is the act of cooperation. This can be difficult at times when the parties involved disagree on fundamental issues of principle. But, there are some things that cannot be accomplished alone and we must work together to get them done. How this cooperation gets organized is a central focus of politics.

Compromise: What makes politics so frustrating is the need for compromise. But, when people differ on basic principles and ideals getting things done requires compromise. Rather than look on this necessity as a flaw of politics we should look on it as an indication of our liberty. Compromise is rarely needed in societies ruled by dictators since they can demand conformity and impose their will without consulting others. The moment we bring other people into the process we introduce the need to compromise. This is an indispensable feature of a free society.

Problem Solving: Of course, the goal of coming together to cooperate and compromise is to solve problems. As a method of problem solving, politics seems impractical and inefficient. But, again we must remember that with liberty comes the ability to disagree and this means that we cannot use the power of politics to impose our will on others. As the Framers of our government recognized, our government is ultimately based on the consent of the governed. The solutions we arrive at for our problems are also ultimately based on this same consent.

A truly informed electorate is necessary to make our political system work at its best and this includes a working knowledge of the system we have. The direct benefits of this come from being better informed voters. But, as with the other subjects we have examined there are also indirect benefits to the study of politics. Our national politics is just a macrocosm of our daily lives where the same need to cooperate, compromise, and solve problems exists. Recognizing this will benefit both realms of life and give us a greater appreciation for the importance of politics.

The Important of Psychology

With the growth of the self-help movement a growing interest in and knowledge of psychology has become common. Given this, it would seem obvious that there are benefits to the study of psychology. But, let's look beyond the obvious benefits to see if there are other aspects of psychology that can give us useful insights.

Self-Help: Clearly the ability to work through one's own emotional difficulties is a useful benefit to the study of psychology. The insights available from the study of psychology are particularly useful in sorting through the various approaches to find one that is most compatible with each individual's needs.

Self-Knowledge: With the rise of self-help has also come the potential to increase one's self knowledge. Indeed, a good knowledge of the self is critical to the successful use of most self-help techniques. Psychology encourages the kind of reflection that one needs in order to gain a better sense of self.

Reason and Feeling: An important benefit to the sty of psychology is the recognition of the distinction between reason and feeling in thinking. While the two function together there is an important difference in their role in thinking. How they are understood separately and how they work together are both often misunderstood and the study of psychology helps to clarify these questions.

Metaphysics: At the root of every approach in psychology is a set of presumptions about how the mind works and how it is related to the brain. Too often this important aspect of the subject is ignored and consequently many people misunderstand the role of the brain in our thinking. While psychology has advanced well beyond the insights of the 17th century philosopher Rene Descartes, many people still have a basically Cartesian dualist view of the mind and the brain. But, there is much that we now know about this subject that is both interesting and useful.

At its most fundamental psychology is the study of the mind and how it works. Given the central importance of thinking and information processing in our world today the benefits of studying psychology are numerous. Given that much of what we think about how we think is wrong the study of psychology is also necessary to correct some of these mistaken intuitions. It is perhaps these less obvious benefits which are the most valuable insights we can gain from the study of psychology.

The Importance of Religion

There are more people who profess a given religion than there are people who actively practice that religion and it also seems to be the case that there are less people who have a working knowledge of religion (both their own and others) than there are people who actively practice a religion. In fact, some studies show that the less religious a person is the more knowledgeable they are about religion in general. But, for those who practice a religion are there any benefits to the study of their own religion? Are there any good reasons to study other religions at all? Let's examine these questions.

Before we begin I must clarify that I am discussing here the benefits of studying religion not practicing religion. The study of religion may be an aid to the practice of religion but the two are not necessarily the same. One can study without practicing and one can practice without studying. Studies have shown that there are numerous benefits to one's mental and physical health that come from the practice of religion. I want to argue that there are also benefits to the study of religion that might be distinct from these.

Tolerance: Many people believe without question that their religion is the correct one and all others are mistaken in important ways. If nothing else the study of religion can foster tolerance towards other beliefs and the people who profess them. In a world with more and more religions being formed all the time this is an important benefit to religious and non-religious people.

Moderation: As Charles Kimball pointed out in his book titled *When Religion Becomes Evil*, problems occur when religious believers take their views as the only right ones and become more extreme in their practice of religion. We have only to look at the events of 9/11 to understand this. But, the study of religion can lead to more moderation in the practice of religion and as a result it becomes less likely that dangerous consequences arise from the practice of religion.

Secularism: While this point is controversial, ultimately the benefit of studying religion as an academic subject is to foster more, not less, secularism. Indeed, studies show that the more people know about religion (their own and others) the less likely they are to actively practice any religion. In other words, the more likely they are to be agnostic or atheist.

Unlike the other subjects examined in this series, the argument I am making here is that the study of the subject leads to less active application of the subject and this is a benefit. But, this is also what makes many people reluctant to take on a serious study of religion. They intuitively recognize that once they learn about other religions and the details of their own, their belief will seem less plausible and they may end up giving it up entirely. But, is this a bad thing? Certainly one can hold fast to a sense of spirituality without holding onto certain beliefs about how the world works that are largely outdated and incorrect. Certainly one can find meaning and purpose in life and live according to a set of ethical principles without appealing to a set of metaphysical presumptions that are largely at odds with what we know about how the world works.

As Carl Sagan pointed out: "In some respects, science has far surpassed religion in delivering awe. How is it that hardly any major religion has looked at science and concluded, 'This is better than we thought! The Universe is much bigger than our prophets said, grander, more subtle, more elegant. God must be even greater than we dreamed!'? Instead they say, 'No, no, no! My god is a little god, and I want him to stay that way.' A religion, old or new, that stressed the magnificence of the Universe as revealed by modern science might be able to draw forth reserves of reverence and awe hardly tapped by the conventional faiths."

The Curriculum

Education

Thomas Sowell	Inside American Education
Ron Ritchart	Intellectual Character
Diane Lopez	Teaching Children
Guy Claxton	Wise Up
Charles Murray	Real Education
William J. Bennett	The Educated Child
Jane Healy	Endangered Minds
Josh Waitzkin	The Art of Learning
Alan Bloom	The Closing of the American Mind
Richard Mitchell	The Graves of Academe
Deanna Kuhn	Education for Thinking
Ellen Galinsky	Mind in the Making
Ken Robinson	Out of Our Minds
Howard Gardner	The Disciplined Mind
	The Unschooled Mind
	Frames of Mind
Jacques Barzun	Begin Here
	Teacher in America
E.D. Hirsch	Cultural Literacy
	The Schools We Need
	The Knowledge Deficit
Oliver Van deMille	A Thomas Jefferson Education
	Jefferson Education Home Companion
Ronald Gross	Peak Learning
	Socrates' Way
Michael Gelb	How to Think Like Leonard da Vinci
	Discover Your Genius
Charlotte Mason	A Philosophy of Education
	School Education
	Home Education

I. Foundations

Language

Wilfred Funk	30 Days to a More Powerful Vocabulary
Barbara Kipfer	Word Nerd
Robert McCrum	The Story of English
William F. Buckley	The Right Word
Leonard Shlain	The Alphabet Versus The Goddess
Lynne Truss	Eats Shoots and Leaves
H.L. Mencken	The American Language
Stephen Miller	Conversation
Simon Winchester	The Professor and the Madman
Lewis Thomas	Etcetera, Etcetera
Steven Pinker	Words and Rules
	The Language Instinct
	The Stuff of Thought
Bill Bryson	The Mother Tongue
	Made in America
Tore Janson	A Natural History of Latin
	Speak
William Safire	Quoth The Maven
	On Language
	Language Maven Strikes Again
	What's The Good Word?
John McWhorter	The Power of Babel
	Doing Our Own Thing
James Boswell	The Life of Samuel Johnson
Ludwig Wittgenstein	Philosophical Investigations

Life Skills

Tom Morris	The Stoic Art of Living
Keith Seddon	Stoic Serenity
Richard Carlson	Don't Sweat The Small Stuff
Reid Buckley	Speaking in Public
P.M. Forni	Choosing Civility
Will Bowen	A Complaint Free World
Pema Chodron	When Things Fall Apart
Carl Honore	In Praise of Slowness
Margaret Lobenstine	The Renaissance Soul
Po Bronson	What Should I Do with My Life?
Neil Cavuto	More Than Money
Thomas Armstrong	The Human Odyssey
Carol Orsborn	The Art of Resilience
Frederic Flach	Resilience
Lawrence Gitman	Fundamentals of Investing
William Poundstone	How Would You Move Mount Fuji?
Albert Ellis	A New Guide to Rational Living
The Dalai Lama	The Art of Happiness
	The Art of Happiness at Work
Viktor Frankl	The Will to Meaning
	Man's Search for Meaning
Stephen Carter	Civility
	Integrity
Alain de Botton	The Consolations of Philosophy
	Status Anxiety
Martin Seligman	Learned Optimism
	Authentic Happiness
Al Siebert	The Survivor Personality
	The Resiliency Advantage
Elliot Cohen	What Would Aristotle Do?
	The New Rational Therapy

Mathematics

Jan Gullberg	Mathematics
Mario Livio	The Golden Ratio
Bulent Atalay	Math and the Mona Lisa
Martin Gardner	Mathematical Puzzles & Diversions
George Polya	How to Solve It
Gottlob Frege	The Foundations of Arithmetic
David Berlinski	A Tour of the Calculus
Robert Kaplan	The Nothing That is
Edward Frenkel	Love and Math
Harry Lorayne	Miracle Math
Scott Flansburg	Math Magic
Tony Crilly	50 Mathematical Ideas
Ian Stewart	Why Beauty is Truth
Sylvia Nasar	A Beautiful Mind
John Casti	Godel A Life of Logic
Ernest Nagel	Godel's Proof
Mark Ryan	Everyday Math for Everyday Life
Andrew Hodges	Alan Turing: The Enigma
	One to Nine
John Allen Paulos	Innumeracy
	Beyond Innumeracy
Amir Aczel	Descartes' Secret Notebook
	The Mystery of the Aleph
	Fermat's Last Theorem
	A Strange Wilderness
Euclid	The Elements
Archimedes	Works
Apollonius	Conics
Nicomachus	Introduction to Arithmetic
Rene Descartes	Geometry
Isaac Newton	Principia

Thinking

Michael Shermer	Why People Believe Weird Things
Theodore Schick	How to Think About Weird Things
D.Q. McInerny	Being Logical
Anthony Weston	Creativity for Critical Thinkers
Jamie Whyte	Crimes Against Logic
Malcolm Gladwell	Blink
Ori Brafman	Sway
Rosalene Glickman	Optimal Thinking
Rolf Dobelli	The Art of Thinking Clearly
Carol Tavris	Mistakes Were Made
Bart Kosko	Fuzzy Thinking
Vincent Ruggiero	Beyond Feelings
Gary Kirby	Thinking
Steven Levitt	Think Like a Freak
Lewis Wolpert	Six Impossible Things Before Breakfast
Ronald Gross	Socrates' Way
Dan Ariely	Predictably Irrational
	The Upside of Irrationality
John Stossel	Myths, Lies, and Downright Stupidities Give Me a Break
Robert Sternberg	The Triarchic Mind
	Thinking Styles
	Successful Intelligence
Aristotle	Logic

II. Moral Philosophy

Economics

Henry Hazlitt	Economics in One Lesson
Tom Harford	The Logic of Life
Robert Frank	The Economic Naturalist
Michael Shermer	The Mind of the Market
Frederic Bastiat	Economic Fallacies
Lawrence Gitman	Fundamentals of Investing
Juliet Schor	The Overspent American
Barry Schwartz	The Paradox of Choice
Richard Conniff	The Natural History of the Rich
Ted Klontz	The Financial Wisdom of Scrooge
Hunter Lewis	Where Keynes Went Wrong
Jim Cox	The Concise Guide to Economics
David Gordon	Economic Reasoning
Steven Levitt	Freakonomics
	Super Freakonomics
George Gilder	Wealth and Poverty
	The Spirit of Enterprise
Mark Skousen	Economics on Trial
	The Power of Economic Thinking
	The Making of Modern Economics
	Economic Logic
Thomas Sowell	Basic Economics
	Applied Economics
	Knowledge and Decisions
F.A. Hayek	The Road to Serfdom
	The Fatal Conceit
Adam Smith	The Wealth of Nations
Ludwig von Mises	Socialism

Ethics

James Rachels	The Elements of Moral Philosophy
James Q. Wilson	The Moral Sense
Robert Wright	The Moral Animal
Randy Cohen	The Good The Bad and the Difference
Michael Shermer	The Science of Good and Evil
Anita Allen	The New Ethics
The Dalai Lama	Ethics for the New Millennium
David Callahan	The Cheating Culture
Rita Manning	A Practical Guide to Ethics
Alasdair MacIntyre	After Virtue
James Hunter	The Death of Character
Matt Ridley	The Origin of Virtue
Marc Hauser	Moral Minds
Elliot Sober	Unto Others
Sam Harris	The Moral Landscape

Plato	The Republic
Aristotle	Nicomachean Ethics
G.E. Moore	Principia Ethica
W.D. Ross	The Right and The Good
J.S. Mill	Utilitarianism
Immanuel Kant	The Critique of Practical Reason

Philosophy

Ed Miller	Questions That Matter
Jerome Shaffer	Reality Knowledge and Value
James Rachels	Problems From Philosophy
Nigel Warburton	Philosophy: The Classics
Diane Collinson	Fifty Major Philosophers
Mortimer Adler	Ten Philosophical Mistakes
Plato	Dialogues
Aristotle	Metaphysics
Rene Descartes	Meditations on First Philosophy
Immanuel Kant	Critique of Pure Reason
Benedict Spinoza	Ethics
Gottfried Leibniz	Monadology
George Berkeley	The Principles of Human Knowledge
Martin Heidegger	Being and Time
Jean Paul Sartre	Being and Nothingness
Thomas Nagel	The View from Nowhere
Gilbert Ryle	The Concept of Mind
Ludwig Wittgenstein	Philosophical Investigations
A.J. Ayer	Language Truth and Logic
Owen Flanagan	The Problem of the Soul
	The Really Hard Problem
David Hume	Enquiry Concerning Human Understanding
John Locke	Essay Concerning Human Understanding
John Austin	Sense and Sensibilia
	Philosophical Papers

Applied Philosophy

Roger-Pol Droit	Astonish Yourself!
Julian Baggini	The Pig That Wants to be Eaten
Peg Tittle	What If...
Marietta McCarty	How Philosophy Can Save Your Life
Pierre Hadot	Philosophy as a Way of Life
Ronald Gross	Socrates' Way
Lou Marinoff	Plato, Not Prozac!
	The Big Questions
	The Middle Way
Elliot Cohen	What Would Aristotle Do?
	The New Rational Therapy
	Philosophers at Work
Christopher Phillips	Socrates Café
	Six Questions of Socrates
	Socrates in Love
Alain de Botton	The Consolations of Philosophy
	Status Anxiety
Thomas Cathcart	Plato and a Platypus Walk into a Bar
	Heidegger and a Hippo
	Aristotle and an Aardvark
Plato	Dialogues
Marcus Aurelius	Meditations
Epictetus	The Discourses

Politics

Howard Fineman	The Thirteen Arguments
John Stuart Mill	On Liberty
George F. Will	Statecraft as Soulcraft
Richard Brookhiser	What Would the Founders Do?
Newt Gingrich	Real Change
John Locke	Second Treatise on Government
Charles Murray	What it Means to Be a Libertarian
	Losing Ground
	In Pursuit of Happiness
Thomas Sowell	The Vision of the Anointed
	The Quest for Cosmic Justice
Alexis Tocqueville	Democracy in America
Baron Montesquieu	The Spirit of Laws
Robert Nozick	Anarchy, State, and Utopia
John Rawls	A Theory of Justice
Plato	Republic
Aristotle	Politics

The Federalist Papers
The Anti-Federalist Papers

Psychology

Edward Shorter	A History of Psychiatry
David Hothersall	History of Psychology
Morton Hunt	The Story of Psychology
Lauren Slater	Opening Skinner's Box
Carl Zimmer	Soul Made Flesh
Paul Churchland	Matter & Consciousness
Jeffrey Schwartz	The Mind and the Brain
Antonio Damasio	Descartes' Error
Ramachandran	Phantoms in the Brain
Christof Koch	Question for Consciousness
Howard Gardner	Frames of Mind
Timothy Wilson	Strangers to Ourselves
Mark Leary	The Curse of the Self
Kenneth Gergen	The Saturated Self
Mihaly Csikszentmihalyi	The Evolving Self
Drew Leder	The Absent Body
Steven Pinker	The Blank Slate
	How the Mind Works
Martin Seligman	Learned Optimism
	The Optimistic Child
Sigmund Freud	Works
William James	The Principles of Psychology
Gilbert Ryle	The Concept of Mind
Immanuel Kant	The Critique of Pure Reason
David Hume	A Treatise of Human Nature
Joseph Campbell	The Portable Jung

Western Religion

Mircea Eliade	The Sacred and the Profane
Charles Kimball	When Religion Becomes Evil
Paul Tillich	A History of Christian Thought
Bernhard Anderson	Understanding the Old Testament
George Smith	Why Atheism?
S.T. Joshi	Atheism A Reader
Stephen Prothero	Religious Literacy
Robert Wright	The Evolution of God
Benson Bobrick	Wide as the Waters
Adam Nicolson	God's Secretaries
Robert Price	The Reason Driven Life
Frank Mead	Handbook of Denominations
Elaine Pagels	The Origin of Satan
Bruce Shelley	Church History in Plain Language
Gary Greenberg	101 Myths of the Bible
Jaroslav Pelikan	Whose Bible is It?
Jack Miles	God A Biography
Bart Ehrman	The New Testament
	Lost Christianities
	Jesus Interrupted
St. Augustine	On Christian Doctrine
St. Thomas Aquinas	Summa Theologica
Thomas Paine	The Age of Reason
The Bible	

World Religion

Karen Armstrong	Islam A Short History
Jack Maguire	Essential Buddhism
Sogyal Rinpoche	Tibetan Book of Living and Dying
Migene Wippler	Santeria The Religion
Stephen Cope	Yoga and the Quest for the True Self
P. Yogananda	Autobiography of a Yogi
Vine Deloria	God is Red
Kahlil Gibran	The Prophet
Mircea Eliade	From Primitives to Zen
E.A. Wallis Budge	The Gods of the Egyptians
James Frazer	The Golden Bough
Coleman Barks	The Essential Rumi
James Pritchard	The Ancient Near East
Confucius	The Analects
Lao Tzu	Tao Te Ching
The Dalai Lama	The World of Tibetan Buddhism
	The Buddhism of Tibet
	The Meaning of Life

The Bhagavad Gita
The Koran

III. Natural Philosophy

Astronomy

Carl Sagan	Cosmos
Timothy Ferris	Coming of Age in the Milky Way
Donald Goldsmith	The Astronomers
Robert Burnham	Astronomy
Terence Dickinson	Nightwatch
Mary Roach	Packing for Mars
James Connor	Kepler's Witch
Thomas Kuhn	The Copernican Revolution
Kenneth Davis	Don't Know Much About the Universe?
David Filkin	Stephen Hawking's Universe
Stephen Hawking	The Universe in a Nutshell
	A Brief History of Time
	Black Holes and Baby Universes
	The Grand Design
Dava Sobel	The Planets
	A More Perfect Heaven
	Galileo's Daughter
Ptolemy	Almagest
Nicolaus Copernicus	Revolutions of the Heavenly Spheres
Johannes Kepler	Epitome of Copernican Astronomy

Biology

Stephen Jay Gould	Wonderful Life
Steve Olson	Mapping Human History
Bryan Sykes	The Seven Daughters of Eve
Brenda Maddox	Rosalind Franklin
Edward O. Wilson	The Diversity of Life
Matt Ridley	Genome
Keith Thomas	Man and the Natural World
Anna Pavord	The Naming of Names
Colin Tudge	The Tree
Michael Shermer	Why Darwin Matters
Richard Rhodes	John James Audubon
Henry David Thoreau	Walden
Jeffrey Masson	When Elephants Weep
Mark Blumberg	Basic Instinct
Robert Bakker	The Dinosaur Heresies
John Horner	Dinosaur Lives
Bill Bryson	A Walk in the Woods
Niles Eldridge	Reinventing Darwin
Daniel Dennett	Darwin's Dangerous Idea
Richard Dawkins	The Selfish Gene
	The Ancestor's Tale
	Climbing Mount Improbable
	The Greatest Show on Earth
Lewis Thomas	The Fragile Species
	The Lives of a Cell
	The Medusa and the Snail
Henry Hobhouse	Seeds of Change
	Seeds of Wealth
Charles Darwin	The Origin of Species

Chemistry

John Emsley	Nature's Building Blocks
Penny Le Couteur	Napoleon's Buttons
Michael Flannery	Civil War Pharmacy
Fiammetta Rocco	The Miraculous Fever-Tree
Ron Beattie	101 Incredible Experiments
Oliver Sacks	Uncle Tungsten
Hannah Holmes	The Secret Life of Dust
Peter Macinnis	Poisons
Jack Kelly	Gunpowder
Victoria Finlay	Color
Simon Garfield	Mauve
John Emsley	The Elements of Murder
	The 13th Element
Joe Schwartz	The Genie in the Bottle
	Radar, Hula Hoops, and Playful Pigs
	That's The Way The Cookie Crumbles
	Dr. Joe and What You Didn't Know
	The Fly in the Ointment
	Let Them Eat Flax
	Science, Sense and Nonsense

Antoine Lavoisier	Elements of Chemistry
Jean Fourier	Analytical Theory of Heat
Michael Faraday	Experimental Researches In Electricity
William Gilbert	On the Loadstone and Magnetism

Geology/Geography

Simon Winchester	The Map That Changed the World
Dava Sobel	Longitude
Stephen Pumfrey	Latitude
Eric Weiner	The Geography of Bliss
William Ryan	Noah's Flood
Peter Clayton	Seven Wonders of the Ancient World
Dennis Dean	Hutton and the History of Geology
Suzanne Staubach	Clay
Alice Outwater	Water
Matthew Hart	Diamond
Victoria Finlay	Jewels
Amir Aczel	The Riddle of the Compass
Sonia Shah	Crude The Story of Oil
Mark Kurlansky	Salt A World History
Barbara Freese	Coal A Human History
Alan Cutler	The Seashell on the Mountaintop
Kenneth Davis	Don't Know Much About Geography
Richard Fortey	Earth an Intimate History
Mark Stein	How the States Got Their Shapes
Martin Dugard	Farther Than Any Man
	Into Africa

Physics

Roger Jones	Physics for the Rest of Us
Albert Einstein	Relativity
Walter Isaacson	Einstein
Bill Bryson	A Short History of Nearly Everything
Melvyn Bragg	On Giants' Shoulders
Royston Roberts	Serendipity
Jay Ingram	The Velocity of Honey
Roger Highfield	The Physics of Christmas
Richard Rhodes	The Making of the Atomic Bomb
Robert Jungk	Brighter Than a Thousand Suns
Amir Aczel	Entanglement
Richard Feynman	Six Easy Pieces
	Six Not-So-Easy Pieces
	QED
Brian Greene	The Elegant Universe
	The Fabric of the Cosmos
Galileo Galilei	The Two New Sciences

IV. History

Ancient History

Ann Kendall	Everyday Life of the Incas
Lionel Casson	Everyday Life in Ancient Egypt
Jon White	Everyday Life in Ancient Egypt
Adolf Erman	Life in Ancient Egypt
Georges Contenau	Everyday Life in Babylon and Assyria
Jean Bottero	Everyday Life in Ancient Mesopotamia
E.W. Heaton	Everyday Life in Old Testament Times
Michael Grant	The History of Ancient Israel
Bernhard Anderson	Understanding the Old Testament
Arthur Cotterell	Chariot
Donald Redford	Akhenaten: The Heretic King
E.A. Wallis Budge	The Gods of the Egyptians
James Pritchard	The Ancient Near East
Peter Ellis	A Brief History of the Druids
Rodney Castleden	The Making of Stonehenge
Will Durant	Our Oriental Heritage
Peter Clayton	Seven Wonders of the Ancient World
Vicki Leon	Uppity Women of Ancient Times
Peter James	Ancient Inventions
	Ancient Mysteries

Gilgamesh
The Bible

Asian History

Charles Dunn	Everyday Life in Traditional Japan
The Dalai Lama	My Land and My People
Jack Weatherford	Genghis Khan
Will Durant	Our Oriental Heritage
Thomas Laird	The Story of Tibet
John Keay	China A History
Stanley Wolpert	A New History of India
Laurence Wu	Fundamentals of Chinese Philosophy
Wing-Tsit Chan	A Source Book in Chinese Philosophy
Alan Watts	The Spirit of Zen
Lizzie Collingham	Curry A tale of Cooks and Conquerors
Santha Rama Rau	The Cooking of India
Rafael Steinberg	The Cooking of Japan
	Pacific and Southeast Asian Cooking
Santideva	Guide to Bodhisattva Way of Life
Confucius	The Analects
Lao Tzu	Tao Te Ching
I Ching	
Bhagavad Gita	

Greece & Rome

Thomas Cahill	Sailing the Wine-Dark Sea
F.R. Cowell	Life in Ancient Rome
Lionel Casson	Everyday Life in Ancient Rome
Robert Flaceliere	Daily Life in Greece
A.C. Bouquet	Everyday Life in New Testament Times
Frederick Copleston	A History of Philosophy Volume I
Michael Grant	K The Fall of the Roman Empire
	The Classical Greeks
	The Climax of Rome
Will Durant	The Life of Greece
	Caesar and Christ
G.E.R. Lloyd	Early Greek Science
	Greek Science After Aristotle
Tacitus	The Annals & The Histories
Plutarch	Lives of Noble Grecians & Romans
Herodotus	The History
Thucydides	The History of Peloponnesian War
Suetonius	Lives of the Twelve Caesars
Edward Gibbon	Decline and Fall of Roman Empire
Plato	The Republic
Epictetus	Discourses
Marcus Aurelius	Meditations

The Middle Ages

Robert Lacey	The Year 1000
Danny Danziger	1215 The Year of the Magna Carta
Morris Bishop	The Middle Ages
Andrew Bridgeford	1066
Richard Dales	Scientific Achievement of Middle Ages
Marjorie Rowling	Life in Medieval Times
Jack Weatherford	Genghis Khan
Albert Hourani	A History of the Arab Peoples
Christiane Zuber	A History of Women
Will Durant	The Age of Faith
Prudence Jones	A History of Pagan Europe
Andrew McCall	The Medieval Underworld
Michael Paine	The Crusades
Hugh Soar	The Crooked Stick
Barbara Tuchman	A Distant Mirror
Vicki Leon	Uppity Women of Medieval Times
Christopher Dyer	Everyday Life in Medieval England
Sherrilyn Kenyon	Everyday Life in the Middle Ages
Frances Gies	Women in the Middle Ages
Joseph Gies	Life in a Medieval Castle
	Life in a Medieval Village
Frederick Copleston	History of Philosophy Volume II
	History of Philosophy Volume III

Geoffrey Chaucer	The Canterbury Tales
Dante	The Divine Comedy

The Middle East

Albert Hourani	A History of the Arab Peoples
Michael Grant	The History of Ancient Israel
Brian Murphy	The Root of Wild Madder
Christopher Kremmer	The Carpet Wars
Sir John Glubb	History of the Arab People
Karen Armstrong	Islam A Short History
Andrew Mango	Ataturk
Stewart Allen	The Devil's Cup
Michael Paine	The Crusades
Bernard Lewis	The Middle East
Jacob Fellure	The Middle East
Malise Ruthven	Islam in The World
Harry Nickles	Middle Eastern Cooking
Georges Contenau	Everyday Life In Babylon
Jean Bottero	Everyday Life Mesopotamia
A.C. Bouquet	Everyday Life in New Testament Times
E.W. Heaton	Everyday Life in Old Testament Times

The Quran	
Edward Fitzgerald	Rubaiyat of Omar Khayyam
Kabir	Ecstatic Poems

Renaissance History

Arthur Herman	How Scots Invented the Modern World
A.L. Rowse	The Elizabethan Renaissance
Liza Picard	Elizabeth's London
Serge Bramly	Leonardo
Fritjof Capra	The Science of Leonardo
Michael Wood	Shakespeare
Will Durant	The Renaissance
Allen Debus	Man and Nature in the Renaissance
Vicki Leon	Women of Shakespearean Times
Charles Mann	1491
Bernard Williams	Descartes The Project of Pure Enquiry
Thomas Kuhn	The Copernican Revolution
James Connor	Kepler's Witch
Dava Sobel	A More Perfect Heaven
	Galileo's Daughter

Michel de Montaigne	The Essays
Nicolo Machiavelli	The Prince
Francois Rabelias	Gargantua and Pantagruel
William Shakespeare	Works
Marsilio Ficino	Meditations on the Soul
Leonardo da Vinci	Notebooks
Francis Bacon	Advancement of Learning
	Novum Organum
Rene Descartes	Meditations
	Discourse on Method

English History

Walter Houghton	The Victorian Frame of Mind
Danny Danziger	1215 The Year of the Magna Carta
Richard Altick	Victorian People and Ideas
Judith Flanders	Inside the Victorian Home
N.G. Pounds	The Culture of the English People
Daniel Pool	What Jane Austen Ate
Jessica Warner	Craze
Martin Wallace	A Short History of Ireland
Jenny Uglow	A History of British Gardening
A.L. Rowse	The Elizabethan Renaissance
Pantagenet Fry	Kings and Queens of England
Amanda Vickery	The Gentleman's Daughter
Dorothy Marshall	English People in the 18th Century
Maureen Waller	1700 Scenes from London Life
Edgar Vincent	Nelson Love & Fame
Michael Wood	Shakespeare
Christopher Hibbert	Wellington A Personal History
J.S. Mill	On Liberty
David Hume	Essays
John Locke	Second Treatise on Government
Lord Acton	Essays in Religion, Politics, Morality
	Essays in the History of Liberty
	Essays in the Study of History
William Manchester	The Last Lion Volume I
	The Last Lion Volume II
Liza Picard	Dr. Johnson's London
	Elizabeth's London
Simon Schama	A History of Britain I
	A History of Britain II
	A History of Britain III

Modern European History

Charles Esdaile	The Peninsular War
Jasper Ridley	The Freemasons
Allen Brown	The Origins of Modern Europe
Jeffry Kaplow	New Perspectives on French Revolution
Jay Winik	The Great Upheaval
Pieter Geyl	Napoleon For & Against
Max Lenz	Napoleon
Mike Rapport	1848
Thomas Paine	The Rights of Man
John Locke	Second Treatise on Government
J.J. Rousseau	The Social Contract
Frederich Coppleston	History of Philosophy Volume IV
	History of Philosophy Volume V
	History of Philosophy Volume VI
	History of Philosophy Volume VII
Will Durant	The Reformation
	The Age of Reason Begins
	The Age of Louis XIV
	The Age of Napoleon
	The Age of Voltaire
	Rousseau and Revolution

American History I

William Bennett	America The Last Best Hope Volume 1
George Dow	Everyday Life in Ma. Bay Colony
Carol Holliday	Woman's Life in Colonial Days
Alice Earle	Child Life in Colonial Days
David Hawke	Everyday Life in Early America
Bruce Daniels	Puritans at Play
John Demos	A Little Commonwealth
Virginia Anderson	Creatures of Empire
Dale Taylor	Everyday Life in Colonial America
John Alden	A History of the American Revolution
Richard Brookhiser	Founding Father
R.B. Bernstein	Thomas Jefferson
Fawn Brodie	Thomas Jefferson
Joseph Ellis	Founding Brothers
James Burke	American Connections
Stephen Ambrose	Undaunted Courage
William Miller	The Business of May Next
Thomas Paine	Common Sense
Ron Chernow	Alexander Hamilton
Marla Miller	Betsy Ross
David McCullough	1776
	John Adams
Walter Isaacson	Benjamin Franklin
	A Benjamin Franklin Reader

Letters of Abigail and John Adams
Declaration of Independence
U.S. Constitution
Federalist Papers

American History II

William Bennett	America The Last Best Hope Volume I
Geoffrey Ward	The Civil War
Henry Commager	The Civil War Archive
James McPherson	Battle Cry of Freedom
Bruce Catton	The Civil War
Shelby Foote	The Civil War
Michael Varhola	Everyday Life During the Civil War
Marc McCutcheon	Everyday Life in the 1800s
Robert Walker	Everyday Life in the Age of Enterprise
Michael Flannery	Civil War Pharmacy
Jacqueline Tobin	Hidden in Plain View
Paul Boller	American Transcendentalism
Michael Dolan	The American Porch
Louis Menand	The Metaphysical Club
Dee Brown	Bury My Heart at Wounded Knee
Christopher Corbett	Orphans Preferred
Candy Moulton	Everyday Life in the Wild West
	Everyday Life Among American Indians

Ralph W. Emerson	Essays
Henry D. Thoreau	Walden
William James	Pragmatism
Herman Melville	Moby Dick
Nathanial Hawthorne	The Scarlet Letter
Stephen Crane	The Red Badge of Courage
Edgar Allen Poe	Short Stories and Poems
Mark Twain	Adventures of Huckleberry Finn
Alexis de Tocqueville	Democracy in America

American History III

William Bennett	America The Last Best Hope Volume II
Dinesh D'Souza	What's so Great About America
David Kyvig	Daily Life in the U.S. 1920-1940
Frederick Allen	Only Yesterday
John Woods	Everyday Life in 20th Century
David Brinkley	Washington Goes to War
Thomas Friedman	The World is Flat
Paul Johnson	A History of The American People
Whittaker Chambers	Witness
Robert Sobel	Coolidge
David McCullough	Truman
Meryle Secrest	Frank Lloyd Wright
A. Scott Berg	Lindbergh
Neil Baldwin	Edison
Mark Kurlansky	1968
	Food of a Younger Land
Edmund Morris	Theodore Rex
	Dutch
Henry Kissinger	Diplomacy
	Does America Need a Foreign Policy?

20th Century History

Richard Pipes	The Russian Revolution
Henry Kissenger	Diplomacy
Whittaker Chambers	Witness
Mark Kurlansky	1968
Frederick Allen	Only Yesterday
Edmund Morris	Dutch
David McCullough	Truman
Peter Watson	The Modern Mind
Barbara Tuchman	The Guns of August
Anne Frank	Diary
Richard Rhodes	The Making of the Atomic Bomb
John Dodds	Everyday Life in 20th Century America
Frederick Copleston	History of Philosophy Volume VIII
	History of Philosophy Volume IX
William Manchester	The Last Lion Volume 1
	The Last Lion Volume 2
H.L. Mencken	Vintage Mencken
	Prejudices
	Chrestomathy
	A Second Chrestomathy
	The American Scene
	35 Years of Newspaper Work
William F. Buckley	The Fall of the Berlin Wall
	On the Firing Line
	A Hymnal
	Execution Eve
	Inveighing We Will Go
	Right Reason
	The Governor Listeth
	Happy Days Were here Again
	Up From Liberalism
	Rumbles Left and Right

Women in History

Louann Brizendine	The Female Brain
Sara Shandler	Ophelia Speaks
Betty Friedan	The Feminine Mystique
Mona Schulz	The New Feminine Brain
Antonia Fraser	The Warrior Queens
Frances Gies	Women in the Middle Ages
Jean Bolen	Goddesses in Everywoman
Merlin Stone	When God was a Woman
Natalie Angier	Woman An Intimate Geography
Carol Holliday	Woman's Life in Colonial Days
Leonard Shlain	Sex, Time and Power
George Scott	The History of Prostitution
Christiane Zuber	A History of Women
Betsy Prioleau	Seductress
Amanda Foreman	Georgianna
Marla Miller	Betsy Ross
Brenda Maddox	Rosalind Franklin
Katie Hickman	Courtesans
Bryan Sykes	The Seven Daughters of Eve
	Adam's Curse
Vicki Leon	Women of Shakespearean Times
	Uppity Women of Medieval Times
	Uppity Women of Ancient Times
Marilyn Yalom	A History of the Breast
	A History of the Wife
Rosalind Miles	Guenevere
	Who Cooked the Last Supper?

World History

Michael Cook	A Brief History of the Human Race
Jacques Barzun	From Dawn to Decadence
John Garraty	The Columbia History of the World
Richard Tarnas	The Passion of the Western Mind
Charles van Doren	A History of Knowledge
Howard Gardner	Creating Minds
Charles Murray	Human Accomplishment
Clive James	Cultural Amnesia
Daniel Boorstin	The Creators
Harold Bloom	Genius
Robert Wright	Nonzero
Michael Olmert	Milton's Teeth and Ovid's Umbrella
Hannah Holmes	The Secret Life of Dust
Barbara Tuchman	The March of Folly
Stephen Mason	A History of the Sciences
Barbara Ehrenreich	Blood Rites
Jack Kelly	Gunpowder
Robert Bernstein	Sparks of Genius
Michael Gelb	Discover Your Genius
Jared Diamond	Guns, Germs, and Steel
	Collapse
Thomas Sowell	Conquest & Cultures
	Migration & Cultures
	Race & Culture
James Burke	The Day the Universe Changed
	Circles
	The Knowledge Web
	The Pinball Effect
G.W.F. Hegel	Philosophy of History

V. Humanities

Art

Leonard Shlain	Art & Physics
Victoria Finlay	Color
Amy Greenfield	A Perfect Red
Phyllis Bober	Art, Cuisine, & Culture
Michel Pastoureau	Blue The History of a Color
Ellen Langer	On Becoming an Artist
Jacob Hobbs	Arts, Ideas, and Civilization
Paul Johnson	Art A New History
Alberto Manguel	Reading Pictures
Anthony Janson	History of Art
Alain de Botton	Art as Therapy
Edmund Swinglehurst	Salvador Dali
David Larkin	Frank Lloyd Wright
Maria Costantino	Frank Lloyd Wright Design
Stephen Farthing	1001 Paintings You Must See
Kristina Lewis	50 Paintings You Should Know
Howard Gardner	Arts & Human Development
	Art, Mind, and Brain

Literature

Johann Goethe	Faust
Leo Tolstoy	War and Peace
Miguel Cervantes	Don Quixote
Henry Fielding	Tom Jones
Jonathan Swift	Gulliver's Travels
Laurence Sterne	Tristram Shandy
Francois Rabelais	Gargantua and Pantagruel
Dante	The Divine Comedy
Geoffrey Chaucer	Canterbury Tales
Aldous Huxley	Brave New World
Alexandre Dumas	The Man in the Iron Mask
Charlotte Bronte	Jane Eyre
Victor Hugo	The Hunchback of Notre Dame
Herman Melville	Moby Dick
Robert Louis Stevenson	Treasure Island
Daniel Defoe	Robinson Crusoe
Virgil	The Aeneid
Homer	The Iliad
	The Odyssey
Franz Kafka	The Castle
	The Trial
Fyodor Dostoevsky	The Brothers Karamazov
	Crime and Punishment
Charles Dickens	Our Mutual Friend
	Great Expectations
	Oliver Twist
	David Copperfield
	The Pickwick Papers
Jane Austen	Pride and Prejudice
	Persuasion
	Mansfield Park
	Sense and Sensibility

Music

Daniel Levitin	This is Your Brain on Music
John Szwed	Jazz 101
Thomas Levenson	Measure for Measure
Richard Florida	Rise of the Creative Class
Mihaly Csikszentmihalyi	Creativity
Oliver Sacks	Musicophilia
Russell Martin	Beethoven's Hair
A.C. Kalischer	Beethoven's Letters
Philip Glass	Music by Philip Glass
Rollo Meyers	Erik Satie
Arnold Schoenberg	Theory of Harmony
Wolfgang Hildesheimer	Mozart A Biography
Don Campbell	The Mozart Effect
Harrison Wighall	In Mozart's Footsteps
Catherine Kendall	More Stories of Composers
Harold Schoenberg	The Great Pianists
Leonice Kidd	They All Sat Down
H.C. Landon	The Mozart Essays
Anthony Storr	Music and the Mind
Howard Gardner	Creating Minds
James Austin	Chase, Chance, and Creativity
Mary-Elaine Jacobsen	The Gifted Adult
Ellen Langer	On Becoming an Artist
Phil Goulding	Classical Music
	Ticket to the Opera

Plays

Aeschylus	The Plays
Sophocles	The Plays
Euripides	The Plays
Aristophanes	The Plays
William Shakespeare	The Plays
Henrik Ibsen	The Plays
T.S. Eliot	The Plays
Jean-Paul Sartre	The Plays
Samuel Beckett	The Plays
Athold Fugard	The Plays
Eugene O'Neill	The Plays
Tennessee Williams	The Plays
Ken Ludwig	Teach Your Children Shakespeare
Michael Macrone	Brush up on Your Shakespeare

Poetry

Edward Fitzgerald	Rubaiyat of Omar Khayyam
John Milton	Paradise Lost
Edna St. Vincent Millay	Collected Lyrics
T.S. Eliot	The Complete Poems
William Shakespeare	Sonnets
Alfred Tennyson	Poems
Henry Longfellow	Poems
Lord Byron	Poems
Robert Browning	Poems
Edgar Allen Poe	Poems
Kabir	Ecstatic Poems
Rabindranath Tagore	Fireflies
Rainer Maria Rilke	Poems
Emily Dickenson	Poems
Friedrich Holderlin	Poems
Robert Frost	Poems
William Blake	Poems
Christopher Marlowe	Poems
Dante	The Divine Comendy
Virgil	The Aeneid
Homer	The Iliad
	The Odyssey

VI. Other

Biography

David Nasaw	Andrew Carnegie
A. Scott Berg	Charles Lindbergh
Miles Davis	Miles Davis
Thomas Blass	Stanley Milgram
Sylvia Nasar	John Nash
Serge Bramly	Leonardo
Ron Chernow	Alexander Hamilton
Annie Cohen-Solal	Jean Paul Sartre
William Manchester	Winston Churchill
Ray Monk	Ludwig Wittgenstein
John Keane	Thomas Paine
Andrew Hodges	Alan Turing
Marla Miller	Betsy Ross
Meryle Secrest	Frank Lloyd Wright
Sydney Kirkpatrick	Edgar Cayce
Neil Baldwin	Thomas Edison
Amanda Foreman	Georgiana
Peter Ackroyd	William Blake
Edgar Vincent	Horatio Nelson
Christopher Hibbert	Wellington
Marvin Kalb	Henry Kissinger
Harold Bloom	William Shakespeare
The Dalai Lama	The Dalai Lama
Sam Tanenhaus	Whittaker Chambers
Gregory Wolfe	Malcolm Muggeridge
John Judis	William F. Buckley
Douglas Stenerson	H.L. Mencken
Fawn Brodie	Joseph Smith
Clive James	Cultural Amnesia
Harold Bloom	William Shakespeare
	Genius
Walter Isaacson	Benjamin Franklin
	Albert Einstein

Buddhism

Jack Maguire	Essential Buddhism
Thubten Chodron	Buddhism for Beginners
Traleg Kyabgon	The Essence of Buddhism
Santideva	Guide to Bodhisattva Way of Life
C.N. Hu	Zen
Alan Watts	The Spirit of Zen
Sogyal Rinpoche	Tibetan Book of Living and Dying
Shunryu Suzuki	Zen Mind, Beginner's Mind
Rick Hanson	Buddha's Brain
Thich Nhat Hanh	The Heart of the Buddha's Teaching
Pema Chodron	No Time to Lose
Lama Surya Das	Buddha is as Buddha Does
	Awakening the Buddhist Heart
	Awakening the Buddha Within
The Dalai Lama	The World of Tibetan Buddhism
	The Buddhism of Tibet
	Essential Teachings
	The Meaning of Life

The Civil War

Bruce Catton	The Civil War
Edward Stackpole	They Met at Gettysburg
Michael Flannery	Civil War Pharmacy
Geoffrey Ward	The Civil War
Shelby Foote	The Civil War
Gene Smith	Lee and Grant
A.L. Long	Memoirs of Robert E. Lee
James McPherson	Battle Cry of Freedom
Michael Varhola	Everyday Life During the Civil War
George Stewart	Pickett's Charge
James Longstreet	From Manassas to Appomattox
Douglas Freeman	Lee's Lieutenants Volumes 1-3
Ned Bradford	Battles and Leaders of the Civil War
Richard Harwell	The Union Reader
	The Confederate Reader
Henry Commager	The Blue and The Gray
	The Civil War Archive
Burke Davis	To Appomattox
	Gray Fox
	Jeb Stuart The Last Cavalier
	They Called Him Stonewall

Death

Alan Segal	Life After Death
Gary Schwartz	The Afterlife Experiments
Frank Tipler	The Physics of Immortality
Robert Wilkins	Death
James Hillman	The Force of Character
Deepak Chopra	Life After Death
Bruce Reichenbach	Is Man The Phoenix?
Terence Penelhum	Immortality
Raymond Moody	Life After Life
Antony Flew	Merely Mortal?
David Skal	Death Makes a Holiday
The Dalai Lama	Advice on Dying
Stephen Prothero	Purified by Fire
Robert Almeder	Death and Personal Survival
Elisabeth Kubler-Ross	On Death and Dying
	Life Lessons
Mary Roach	Spook
	Stiff

Everyday Life

Jean Bottero	Everyday Life in Ancient Mesopotamia
Anne Pearson	Everyday Life in Ancient Greece
Michael Varhola	Everyday Life During the Civil War
John Dodds	Everyday Life in Twentieth Century
George Dow	Everyday Life in the Mass. Bay Colony
Robert Walker	Everyday Life The Age of Enterprise
Marc McCutcheon	Everyday Life in the 1800s
David Hawke	Everyday Life in Early America
Christopher Dyer	Everyday Life in Medieval England
John White	Everyday Life in Ancient Egypt
Ann Kendal	Everyday Life of the Incas
Kristine Hughes	Everyday Life in England
A.C. Bouquet	Everyday Life in New Testament Times
E.W. Heaton	Everyday Life in Old Testament Times
Liza Picard	Everyday Life in Elizabethan London
Georges Contenau	Everyday Life in Babylon & Assyria
Charles Dunn	Everyday Life in Traditional Japan
Sherrilyn Kenyhon	Everyday Life in the Middle Ages
Dale Taylor	Everyday Life in Colonial America
Marjorie Rowling	Life in Medieval Times
Carl Holliday	Woman's Life in Colonial Days
F.R. Cowell	Life in Ancient Rome
Adolf Erman	Life in Ancient Egypt
Robert Flaceliere	Daily Life in Greece
David Kyvig	Daily Life in the US 1920-1940
Alice Earle	Child Life in Colonial Days
Marjorie Quennell	Everyday Life in Norman Times
Lionel Casson	Everyday Life in Ancient Egypt
	Everyday Life in Ancient Rome
Candy Moulton	Everyday Life in the Wild West
	Everyday Life Among the Indians
Frances Gies	Life in a Medieval Village
	Life in a Medieval Castle

Food

Martin Jones	Feast
Sue Shephard	Pickled, Potted, and Canned
Walter Gratzer	Terrors of the Table
Michael Pollan	The Omnivore's Dilemma
Kenneth Kiple	A Movable Feast
Laura Shapiro	Something from the Oven
Nichola Fletcher	Charlemagne's Tablecloth
Betty Fussell	The Story of Corn
Felipe Armesto	Near a Thousand Tables
Linda Cilitello	Cuisine and Culture
Phyllis Bober	Art, Culture, and Cuisine
Stephen Mennell	All Manners of Food
Brian Fagan	Fish on Friday
Reay Tannahill	Food in History
Maguelonne Toussaint	History of Food
Inga Saffron	Caviar
Larry Zuckerman	The Potato
Patricia Rain	Vanilla
H.E. Jacob	Six Thousand Years of Bread
Joe Schwarcz	Let Them Eat Flax
Andrew Smith	Peanuts
Don Voorhees	Why Does Popcorn Pop?
	Why Do Donuts Have Holes?
Mort Rosenblum	Olives
	Chocolate
Margaret Visser	The Rituals of Dinner
	Much Depends on Dinner
Mark Kurlansky	Cod
	Salt A World History
	The Big Oyster
	Food of a Younger Land

General Science

Theodore Schick — How to Think About Weird Things
Jay Ingram — The Velocity of Honey
Penny Le Couteur — Napoleon's Buttons
Melvyn Bragg — On Giants' Shoulders
Royston Roberts — Serendipity
Stephen Mason — A History of the Sciences
Peter Smith — Theory and Reality
E.D. Klemke — Philosophy of Science
Edward O. Wilson — Consilience
Stephen Jay Gould — The Hedgehog, Fox, and Magister's Pox
Paul Feyerabend — Against Method
Thomas Kuhn — The Structure of Scientific Revolutions
Karl Popper — The Logic of Scientific Discovery
Michael Shermer — The Borderlands of Science
Science Friction
Joe Schwarcz — Let Them Eat Flax
The Genie in the Bottle
Radar, Hula Hoops, and Playful Pigs
That's The Way The Cookie Crumbles
Dr. Joe and What You Didn't Know

Happiness

Joan Oliver	Happiness
Richard Schoch	The Secret of Happiness
Nicholas White	A Brief History of Happiness
Jennifer Hecht	The Happiness Myth
Jonathan Haidt	The Happiness Hypothesis
Michael Argyle	The Psychology of Happiness
Darrin McMahon	Happiness A History
Daniel Gilbert	Stumbling on Happiness
Sonja Lyubomirsky	The How of Happiness
Richard Layard	Happiness
Martin Seligman	Authentic Happiness
B. Alan Wallace	Genuine Happiness
Andrew Weil	Spontaneous Happiness
Sharon Salzberg	The Kindness Handbook
Piero Ferrucci	The Power of Kindness
Will Bowen	A Complaint Free World
Viktor Frankl	Man's Search for Meaning
	Man's Search for Ultimate Meaning
	The Will to Meaning
The Dalai Lama	The Art of Happiness
	The Art of Happiness at Work
Gretchen Rubin	The Happiness Project
	Happier at Home

Health & Beauty

Walter Gratzer	Terrors of the Table
Eric Schlosser	Fast Food Nation
Pierce Howard	Owner's Manual for the Brain
Bradley Wilcox	The Okinawa Program
Isadore Rosenfeld	The Best Treatment
Ray Pawlett	The Handbook of Tai Chi
Joan Budilovsky	Meditation
Bill Moyers	Healing and the Mind
Paul Martin	The Healing Mind
Marion Roach	The Roots of Desire
Naomi Wolf	The Beauty Myth
Angus Trumble	A Brief History of the Smile
Bernd Heinrich	Why We Run
Michael Sims	Adam's Navel
Stephanie Tourles	Organic Body Care Recipes
Daniel McNeill	The Face
Nancy Etcoff	Survival of the Prettiest
Edwin Morris	Fragrance
Dorie Byers	Natural Beauty Basics
Janice Cox	Natural Beauty at Home
	Natural Beauty for All Seasons
Michael Roizen	You The Owner's Manual
	Real Age
Andrew Weil	Health and Healing
	8 Weeks to Optimum Health
Joe Schwarcz	Let Them Eat Flax
	The Way the Cookie Crumbles
	The Genie in the Bottle
	The Fly in the Ointment

Herbalism & Gardening

Varro Tyler	The Honest Herbal
J.T. Garrett	The Cherokee Herbal
Stephen Buhner	Herbal Antibiotics
Mark Blumenthal	Herbal Medicine
Matthew Wood	Vitalism
Amy Stewart	Flower Confidential
Adelma Simmons	Herb Gardening in Five Seasons
Betty Jacobs	Growing and Using Herbs Successfully
Michael Tierra	The Way of Herbs
Richard Mabey	The New Age Herbalist
Marie Miczak	Nature's Weeds, Native Medicine
Alex Berman	America's Botanico-Medical Movements
U.P. Hedrick	Sturtevant's Edible Plants of the World
Richard Hatton	Handbook of Plant & Floral Ornament
Peg Streep	Spiritual Gardening
David Stuart	Dangerous Gardens
Mike Dash	Tulipomania
Anna Pavord	The Tulip
Diane Ackerman	Cultivating Delight
Sharman Russell	Anatomy of a Rose
Gunilla Norris	A Mystic Garden
Brian Capon	Botany for Gardeners
Jenny Uglow	A Little History of British Gardening

Intelligence & Creativity

Charles Murray	The Bell Curve
Daniel Seligman	A Question of Intelligence
Jeremy Narby	Intelligence in Nature
David Perkins	Outsmarting IQ
Stephen Jay Gould	The Mismeasure of Man
Mary-Elaine Jacobsen	The Gifted Adult
Carl Sagan	The Dragons of Eden
Ken Robinson	Out of Our Minds
Tony Wagner	Creating Innovators
Bruce Nussbaum	Creative Intelligence
Michael Michalko	Thinkertoys
Jonah Lehrer	Imagine
Daniel Nettle	Strong Imagination
James Austin	Chase, Chance, and Creativity
Edward de Bono	Creativity Workout
Austin Kleon	Show Your Work!
Daniel Boorstin	The Creators
David Lynch	Catching the Big Fish
Robert Sternberg	The Triarchic Mind
	Thinking Styles
	Successful Intelligence
Daniel Goleman	Social Intelligence
	Emotional Intelligence
Howard Gardner	Intelligence Reframed
	Frames of Mind

Medicine

Julie Fenster	Mavericks, Miracles, and Medicine
William McNeill	Plagues and Peoples
Ina Yalof	The Story of a Hospital
Bertram Bernheim	A Surgeon's Domain
Stuart Zeman	So You Want to be a Doctor...
Noah Fabricant	Why We Became Doctors
Thomas Stern	House Calls
Eric Lax	The Mold in Dr. Florey's Coat
Atul Gawande	Complications
Donald Martin	Referees, Docs and God
Kate Scannell	Death of the Good Doctor
Doctor X	Intern
John McPhee	Heirs of General Practice
Eliza Lo Chin	This Side of Doctoring
Erwin Ackerknecht	A Short History of Medicine
Noga Arikha	Passions and Tempers
Lewis Thomas	The Youngest Science
	The Lives of a Cell
	The Medusa and the Snail
Roy Porter	Quacks
	Madmen
	The Greatest Benefit to Mankind
	Blood and Guts
Hippocrates	Works
Galen	Works

169

Mindfulness

Henry Petroski	Small Things Considered
Ellen Langer	Mindfulness
Andrew Weiss	Beginning Mindfulness
Howard Gardner	Extraordinary Minds
Robert Bernstein	Sparks of Genius
Joan Budilovsky	Meditation
Shakti Gawan	Creative Visualization
Jon Kabat-Zinn	Wherever You Go There You Are
Thich Nhat Hanh	The Miracle of Mindfulness
Leah Cohen	Glass Paper Beans
Ray Pawlett	Handbook of Tai Chi
Guy Claxton	Hare Brain Tortoise Mind
Ronald Gross	Socrates' Way
Michael Gelb	Innovate Like Edison
	How to Think Like da Vinci
The Dalai Lama	Mind in Comfort and Ease
	Stages of Meditation
Mark Epstein	Going to Pieces
	Open to Desire
	Thoughts Without a Thinker

Myth and Magic

Stuart Vyse	Believing in Magic
Elizabeth Barber	When They Severed Earth From Sky
Benson Bobrick	The Fated Sky
Edmund Fuller	Bullfinch's Mythology
J.E. Zimmerman	Dictionary of Classical Mythology
Karen Armstrong	A Short History of Myth
Malcolm Day	100 Characters from Mythology
Keith Thomas	Religion and the Decline of Magic
J.F. Bierlein	Parallel Myths
Elaine Pagels	The Origin of Satan
Kenneth Davis	Don't Know Much About Mythology
James Pritchard	The Ancient Near East
Benson Bobrick	The Fated Sky
Homer	The Odyssey
	The Illiad

Gilgamesh

Parenting

Robert Coles	The Moral Intelligence of Children
Joe Kelly	Dads and Daughters
Robert Brooks	Raising Resilient Children
Lucy Miller	Sensational Kids
Ellen Galinsky	Mind in the Making
Jane Isay	Walking on Eggshells
Martin Seligman	The Optimistic Child
Lee Carol	The Indigo Children
Judith Harris	The Nurture Assumption
Dalton Conley	The Pecking Order
Carl Honore	Under Pressure
Zeynep Biringen	Raising a Secure Child
Robert Shaw	The Epidemic
Dale McGowan	Parenting Beyond Belief
	Raising Freethinkers
William Damon	The Moral Child
	Greater Expectations

Psychology of Religion and God

Pascal Boyer	Religion Explained
Daniel Dennett	Breaking The Spell
Peter Berger	The Sacred Canopy
William James	Varieties of Religious Experience
David Wilson	Darwin's Cathedral
Wayne Oates	The Psychology of Religion
Raymond Paloutzian	The Psychology of Religion
Michael Shermer	How We Believe
Mario Beauregard	The Spiritual Brain
Connie Zweig	The Holy Longing
Basil Mitchell	The Philosophy of Religion
Charles Kimball	When Religion Becomes Evil
Robert Solomon	Spirituality for the Skeptic
Jacob Needleman	Religion for a New Generation
Robert Price	Top Secret
Nicholas Wade	The Faith Instinct
H.L. Mencken	Treatise on the Gods
Jack Miles	God A Biography
Bernard Haisch	The God Theory
Michael Corey	The God Hypothesis
Gerald Schroeder	The Hidden Face of God
Richard Dawkins	The God Delusion
John Hick	The Existence of God
Robert Wright	The Evolution of God
Karen Armstrong	A History of God
Stephen Unwin	The Probability of God
Andrew Newberg	Why God Won't Go Away
	Why We Believe What We Believe

Reading & Writing

Maryanne Wolf	Proust and the Squid
Tom Raabe	Biblioholism
Michael Dirda	Book by Book
Nicholas Basbanes	A Gentle Madness
Leonard Shlain	Alphabet Versus the Goddess
Matthew Battles	Library An Unquiet History
Frederick Lerner	The Story of Libraries
Lionel Casson	Libraries in the Ancient World
Nicholas Basbanes	A Gentle Madness
Steven Fisher	History of Writing
Lewis Thomas	Etcetera, Etcetera
Mortimer Adler	How to Read a Book
Andrew Robinson	The Story of Writing
Alberto Manguel	The Library at Night
	A History of Reading
Henry Petroski	The Book on the Bookshelf
	The Pencil
William Safire	Quoth The Maven
	What's the Good Word

The Senses & The Emotions

Edwin Morris	Fragrance
Patrick Susskind	Perfume
David Abram	The Spell of the Sensuous
Chandler Burr	The Emperor of Scent
Mandy Aftel	Essence and Alchemy
Luca Turin	The Secret of Scent
Diane Ackerman	A Natural History of the Senses
Constance Classon	Aroma
Daniel Levitin	This is Your Brain on Music
Rachel Herz	The Scent of Desire
Scott Cunningham	Magical Aromatherapy
Frank Wilson	The Hand
Stuart Wilson	A Natural History of Emotions
Joanna Bourke	Fear A Cultural History
Jennifer Hecht	Doubt A History
Kay Jamison	Exuberance The Passion for Life
James Bowman	Honor A History
Tom Lutz	Crying
William Irvine	On Desire
Janet Landman	Regret
John Cacioppo	Loneliness
Robert Frank	Passions Within Reason
Paul Ekman	Emotions Revealed
Jean-Paul Sartre	The Emotions
Robert Solomon	True to our Feelings
	The Passions
William Miller	The Anatomy of Disgust
	The Mystery of Courage
Antonio Demasio	Looking for Spinoza
	The Feeling of What Happens
M. Merleau-Ponty	Phenomenology of Perception
	The Primacy of Perception

Sex & Love

Natalie Angier	Woman
Leonard Shlain	Sex, Time and Power
Elizabeth Abbott	A History of Celibacy
Matt Ridley	The Red Queen
Mary Roach	Bonk
Diane Ackerman	A Natural History of Love
David Friedman	A Mind of Its Own
Carol Gilligan	The Birth of Pleasure
Reay Tannahill	Sex in History
Jared Diamond	Why is Sex Fun?
Christopher Phillips	Socrates in Love
Robert Greene	The Art of Seduction
Stephanie Coontz	Marriage A History
Deborah Blum	Sex on the Brain
Thomas Moore	The Soul of Sex
Andrea Hopkins	The Book of Courtly Love
Robert Solomon	Love Emotion, Myth, and Metaphor
	About Love
Marilyn Yalom	A History of the Breast
	A History of the Wife
Helen Fisher	Why We Love
	Anatomy of Love
Plato	Symposium

Sugar & Spice

Jack Turner	Spice
Pat Williard	Secrets of Saffron
Sidney Mintz	Sweetness and Power
Peter Macinnis	Bittersweet
Lizzie Collingham	Curry
Charles Corn	The Scents of Eden
Andrew Dalby	Dangerous Tastes
Pat Willard	Secrets of Saffron
Stewart Allen	The Devil's Cup
Mark Pendergrast	Uncommon Grounds
Alan Macfarlane	The Empire of Tea
Patricia Rain	Vanilla
Joel Brenner	The Emperors of Chocolate
Mort Rosenblum	Chocolate
Sophie Coe	The True History of Chocolate

Time

Carl Honore	In Praise of Slowness
Albert Einstein	Relativity
Philp Zimbardo	The Time Paradox
Martin Heidegger	Being and Time
Stephen Hawking	A Brief History of Time
Jay Griffiths	A Sideways Look at Time
Christopher Dewdney	Acquainted With The Night
David Prerau	Seize the Daylight
David Rast	Music of Silence
John Robinson	Time for Life
David Duncan	Calendar
E.G. Richards	Mapping Time
Ellen Langer	Counter Clockwise
Mihaly Csikszentmihalyi	Finding Flow
Dava Sobel	A More Perfect Heaven
	Longitude

U.S. Presidents

James McPherson	To The Best of My Ability
John Durant	Pictorial History of American Presidents
R.B. Bernstein	Thomas Jefferson
Alf Mapp	Thomas Jefferson
Fawn Brodie	Thomas Jefferson
James Flexner	Washington The Indispensible Man
Thomas Dilorenzo	The Real Lincoln
David Donald	Lincoln
Richard Brookhiser	Founding Father
Robert Sobel	Coolidge: An American Enigma
Jon Meacham	American Lion
Geoffrey Perret	Ulysses S. Grant Soldier & President
Stephen Ambrose	Eisenhower Soldier and President
Peter Collier	The Roosevelts An American Saga
David McCullough	John Adams
	Truman
Edmund Morris	Dutch
	Theodore Rex

Vices

Peter McWilliams	Ain't Nobody's Business if You do
Jessica Warner	Craze
Charles Coulombe	Rum
A.J. Baime	Big Shots
Stuart Walton	Out of It
Tom Standage	History of the World in Six Glasses
Iain Gatley	Tobacco
Dominic Streetfield	Cocaine
Katie Hickman	Courtesans
George Scott	The History of Prostitution
Joseph Epstein	Envy
John Emsley	The Elements of Murder
Tom Lutz	Doing Nothing
Roy Baumeister	Evil
David Schwartz	Roll The Bones
David Callahan	The Cheating Culture
Mark Caldwell	A Short History of Rudeness
Martin Booth	Opium A History
	Cannabis A History

Work

Ricardo Semler	The Seven Day Weekend
Timothy Ferris	The Four Hour Work Week
Alain de Botton	Pleasures and Sorrows of Work
Lisa Gansky	The Mesh
Reid Hoffman	The Startup of You
Kimberly Palmer	The Economy of You
Dan Schawbel	Me 2.0
Seth Godin	The Purple Cow
Thomas Moore	A Life at Work
Thich Nhat Hanh	Work
The Dalai Lama	The Art of Happiness at Work
Mihaly Csikszentmihalyi	Good Business
Claude Whittmeyer	Mindfulness & Meaningful Work
Howard Garner	Good Work
Don Tapscott	Wikinomics
	Macrowikinomics
Dan Pink	To Sell is Human
	Drive
	Free Agent Nation

Reference and Activity Books

Rebecca Rupp	Complete Home Learning Source Book
Norman Willis	Logic Puzzles
Richard Churchill	730 Easy Science Experiments
John Lloyd	The Book of General Ignorance
Rob Beattie	101 Incredible Experiments
Miriam Peskowitz	The Daring Book for Girls
John Lloyd	The Book of General Ignorance
Bill McLain	Do Fish Drink Water?
Karlen Evins	I Didn't Know That
Fabrice Mazza	The Big Book of Riddles
Peg Tittle	What If...
Jessica Pierce	Morality Play
Roger-Pol Droit	Astonish Yourself!
Caryl Krueger	1,444 Fun Things to do With Kids
Julian Baggini	The Pig That Wants to be Eaten
Bernard Grun	The Timetables of History
Trevor Homer	The Book of Origins
Harvey Rachlin	Lucy's Bones, Sacred Stones
Gever Tulley	50 Dangerous Things
Arthur Cotterell	From Aristotle to Zoroaster
David White	Philosophy for Kids
	The Examined Life
E.D. Hirsch	The Dictionary of Cultural Literacy
	Books to Build On
Peter James	Ancient Inventions
	Ancient Mysteries
Don Voorhees	Why do Donuts Have Holes?
	Why Does Popcorn Pop?
William J. Bennett	The Book of Virtues
	The Moral Compass

Astronomy

Astronomy and Empire:
http://www.bbc.co.uk/programmes/p003c1cd

Black Holes:
http://www.bbc.co.uk/programmes/p00547f4

Dark Energy:
http://www.bbc.co.uk/programmes/p003k9g5

Galaxies: http://www.bbc.co.uk/programmes/p003c1cn

The Life of Stars:
http://www.bbc.co.uk/programmes/p00548w8

Mars: http://www.bbc.co.uk/programmes/b00772rr

The Multiverse:
http://www.bbc.co.uk/programmes/b008z744

The Planets:
http://www.bbc.co.uk/programmes/p004y25b

The Poincare Conjecture:
http://www.bbc.co.uk/programmes/p0038x8l

The Universe's Origins:
http://www.bbc.co.uk/programmes/p00545j9

The Universe's Shape:
http://www.bbc.co.uk/programmes/p0054880

The Vacuum of Space:
http://www.bbc.co.uk/programmes/b00jz5t3

Worldwide Telescope:
http://www.worldwidetelescope.org/Home.aspx

Biology

Darwin: On the Origin of Species:
http://www.bbc.co.uk/programmes/b00gd3wy

Darwin: The Voyage of the Beagle:
http://www.bbc.co.uk/programmes/b00gbf2g

Genetics: http://www.bbc.co.uk/programmes/p00547md

Genetic Mutation:
http://www.bbc.co.uk/programmes/b008drvm

Growing up in the Universe:
http://www.ted.com/talks/richard_dawkins_growing_up_in_the_universe.html

Microbiology:
http://www.bbc.co.uk/programmes/b007753d

The Natural Order:
http://www.bbc.co.uk/programmes/p00546ql

The Origins of Life:
http://www.bbc.co.uk/programmes/p004y29f

Encyclopedia of Life: http://www.eol.org/

Visible Body: http://www.visiblebody.com/

Chemistry

Chemical Elements:
http://www.bbc.co.uk/programmes/p00546sz

Oxygen: http://www.bbc.co.uk/programmes/b0088nql

The Science House: http://www.science-house.org/

Molecule of the Month:
http://www.chm.bris.ac.uk/motm/motm.htm

CHEMystery: http://library.thinkquest.org/3659/

Chemistry Education Resources:
http://www.chem1.com/chemed/

Terrific Science: http://www.terrificscience.org/

Economics

I, Pencil: http://www.thefreemanonline.org/featured/i-pencil/

Rinkonomics: http://www.econlib.org/library/Columns/y2006/Kleinorder.html

EconTalk: http://www.econtalk.org/

Economics for the Citizen: http://econfaculty.gmu.edu/wew/misc/econcitizen/index.html

Your Job as Spiritual Work: http://www.researchchannel.org/prog/displayevent.aspx?rID=1990

Origins of Money: http://www.hughlafollette.com/radio/origins.of.money.htm

Ludwig von Mises Institute: http://mises.org/

Common Sense Economics: http://www.commonsenseeconomics.com/

Ethics

The Moral Sense Test:
http://moral.wjh.harvard.edu/index2.html

Morality Play:
http://www.philosophersnet.com/games/morality_play.h
tm

Ethics Bites: http://www.open2.net/ethicsbites/

Ethics Matters: http://ethics.sandiego.edu/

Altruism: http://www.bbc.co.uk/programmes/p0038x9c

Good and Evil:
http://www.bbc.co.uk/programmes/p00545g0

Virtue: http://www.bbc.co.uk/programmes/p005489r

Giraffe Heroes Project: http://www.giraffe.org/

Geology

Ageing the Earth:
http://www.bbc.co.uk/programmes/p005493g

The Cambrian Period:
http://www.bbc.co.uk/programmes/p003k9bg
Earth's Origins:
http://www.bbc.co.uk/programmes/p00547hl

Fossils: http://www.bbc.co.uk/programmes/p00547d3

The KT Boundary:
http://www.bbc.co.uk/programmes/p003k9d0

Oceanography:
http://www.bbc.co.uk/programmes/p00547lb

The Permian-Triassic Boundary:
http://www.bbc.co.uk/programmes/b007r285

Plate Tectonics:
http://www.bbc.co.uk/programmes/b008q0sp

Vulcanology:
http://www.bbc.co.uk/programmes/p005490h

History

Agincourt:
http://www.bbc.co.uk/programmes/p004y25q

The American Century:
http://www.bbc.co.uk/programmes/p0054594

The Black Death:
http://www.bbc.co.uk/programmes/b00bcqt8

Byzantium:
http://www.bbc.co.uk/programmes/p00547j9

Catherine the Great:
http://www.bbc.co.uk/programmes/p003hycx

The Carolingian Renaissance:
http://www.bbc.co.uk/programmes/p003hydz

Constantinople Siege and Fall:
http://www.bbc.co.uk/programmes/p0038xbd

The French Revolution's Legacy:
http://www.bbc.co.uk/programmes/p00547gg

The Glorious Revolution:
http://www.bbc.co.uk/programmes/p00547fk

History and Understanding the Past:
http://www.bbc.co.uk/programmes/p00546qd

History of History:
http://www.bbc.co.uk/programmes/b00gryrx

History's Relevance in the 20th Century:
http://www.bbc.co.uk/programmes/p005458g

Napoleon and Wellington:
http://www.bbc.co.uk/programmes/p00547jy

The Pilgrim Fathers:
http://www.bbc.co.uk/programmes/b007rlb6

Roman Britain:
http://www.bbc.co.uk/programmes/p00548xn

Rome and European Civilization:
http://www.bbc.co.uk/programmes/p00547ms

The Roman Empire's Collapse:
http://www.bbc.co.uk/programmes/p00547ds

The Roman Empire's Decline and Fall:
http://www.bbc.co.uk/programmes/p004y237

The Roman Republic:
http://www.bbc.co.uk/programmes/p004y26w

The Sassanid Empire:
http://www.bbc.co.uk/programmes/b008g2x5

Sparta: http://www.bbc.co.uk/programmes/b00nvz72

Tacitus: http://www.bbc.co.uk/programmes/b00cdtxp

Thermopylae:
http://www.bbc.co.uk/programmes/p004y278

Washington and the American Revolution:
http://www.bbc.co.uk/programmes/p004y28v

Humanities

The Artist:
http://www.bbc.co.uk/programmes/p00548cd

The Baroque Movement:
http://www.bbc.co.uk/programmes/b00fhp85

Beauty: http://www.bbc.co.uk/programmes/p003k9hf

Comedy in Ancient Greek Theatre:
http://www.bbc.co.uk/programmes/p003c1d3

Dante's Inferno:
http://www.bbc.co.uk/programmes/b00f05zj

Dickens: http://www.bbc.co.uk/programmes/p00547hx

The Epic: http://www.bbc.co.uk/programmes/p00548t1

The Greek Myths:
http://www.bbc.co.uk/programmes/b0093z1k

Greek & Roman Love Poetry:
http://www.bbc.co.uk/programmes/b0077744

The Later Romantics:
http://www.bbc.co.uk/programmes/p004y24r

Literary Modernism:
http://www.bbc.co.uk/programmes/p00547fv

The Metaphysical Poets:
http://www.bbc.co.uk/programmes/b00cbqhq

Milton: http://www.bbc.co.uk/programmes/p00548bg

Munch and the Scream:
http://www.bbc.co.uk/programmes/b00rbmrx

The Novel:
http://www.bbc.co.uk/programmes/p005463z

The Odyssey:
http://www.bbc.co.uk/programmes/p004y297

The Oresteia:
http://www.bbc.co.uk/programmes/p003k9fk

Pastoral Literature:
http://www.bbc.co.uk/programmes/p003c1cs

Reading: http://www.bbc.co.uk/programmes/p00546nk

Rhetoric: http://www.bbc.co.uk/programmes/p004y263

The Romantics:
http://www.bbc.co.uk/programmes/p00546ws

Shakespeare and Literary Criticism:
http://www.bbc.co.uk/programmes/p00545dp

Shakespeare's Works:
http://www.bbc.co.uk/programmes/p00546s8

The Sonnet:
http://www.bbc.co.uk/programmes/p00547gy

The Aeneid:
http://www.bbc.co.uk/programmes/p003k9c1

Tragedy: http://www.bbc.co.uk/programmes/p005464v

Mathematics

What are Numbers?
http://www.philosophytalk.org/pastShows/Number.html

Kurt Godel and the Limits of Mathematics:
http://www.abc.net.au/rn/philosopherszone/stories/2010/2814096.htm

Mathematics and Biology:
http://www.ted.com/speakers/steven_strogatz.html

The Times' Sexy Maths column:
http://www.ted.com/speakers/marcus_du_sautoy.html

African Fractals:
http://blog.ted.com/2007/11/ron_eglash.php

Mathematics Unintended Consequences:
http://www.bbc.co.uk/programmes/b00qj2nq

Calculus: http://www.bbc.co.uk/programmes/b00mrfwq
Infinity: http://www.bbc.co.uk/programmes/p0054927

Indian Mathematics:
http://www.bbc.co.uk/programmes/p0038xb0

Lovelace: http://www.bbc.co.uk/programmes/b0092j0x

The Importance of Mathematics:
http://www.bbc.co.uk/programmes/p00545hk

Mathematics and Music:
http://www.bbc.co.uk/programmes/p003c1b9

Negative Numbers:
http://www.bbc.co.uk/programmes/p003hyd9

Pi: http://www.bbc.co.uk/programmes/p004y291

Prime Numbers:
http://www.bbc.co.uk/programmes/p003hyf5

Probability:
http://www.bbc.co.uk/programmes/b00bqf61

Pythagoras:
http://www.bbc.co.uk/programmes/b00p693b

Renaissance Maths:
http://www.bbc.co.uk/programmes/p003k9hq

The Fibonacci Sequence:
http://www.bbc.co.uk/programmes/b008ct2j

Zero: http://www.bbc.co.uk/programmes/p004y254

Philosophy

Radio Free Philosophy:
http://www.wix.com/kyphilosopher/philosopher

Philosophy Talk: http://www.philosophytalk.org

The Philosopher's Magazine:
http://www.philosophersnet.com/

ePhilosopher: http://www.ephilosopher.com/

Meanings of Life: http://www.meaningsoflife.com/

The Guerrilla Radio Show:
http://www.guerrillaradioshow.com/

Closer to Truth: http://www.closertotruth.com/

Common Sense Philosophy:
http://www.bbc.co.uk/programmes/b007qhbn

Empiricism:
http://www.bbc.co.uk/programmes/p004y28g

Existentialism:
http://www.bbc.co.uk/programmes/p00547h8

Logical Positivism:
http://www.bbc.co.uk/programmes/b00lbsj3

Materialism:
http://www.bbc.co.uk/programmes/b009ydlj

Pragmatism:
http://www.bbc.co.uk/programmes/p003k9f5

Stoicism: http://www.bbc.co.uk/programmes/p003k9fs

Physics

Antimatter:
http://www.bbc.co.uk/programmes/b00808w8

Grand Unified Theory:
http://www.bbc.co.uk/programmes/p00546nx

Gravitational Waves:
http://www.bbc.co.uk/programmes/b007h8gv

The Graviton:
http://www.bbc.co.uk/programmes/p003k9ks

The Laws of Motion:
http://www.bbc.co.uk/programmes/b009mvj0

The Measurement Problem in Physics:
http://www.bbc.co.uk/programmes/b00hv1dp

Nuclear Physics:
http://www.bbc.co.uk/programmes/p0054887

The Physics of Reality:
http://www.bbc.co.uk/programmes/p00548dl

The Physics of Time:
http://www.bbc.co.uk/programmes/b00g0nmw

Quantum Gravity:
http://www.bbc.co.uk/programmes/p00547c4

Second law of Thermodynamics:
http://www.bbc.co.uk/programmes/p004y2bm

The Speed of Light:
http://www.bbc.co.uk/programmes/p0038x9h

Psychology

Consciousness:
http://www.bbc.co.uk/programmes/p005464j

Imagination:
http://www.bbc.co.uk/programmes/p00548lc

Imagination and Consciousness:
http://www.bbc.co.uk/programmes/p00546vrb

The Infant brain:
http://www.bbc.co.uk/programmes/b00r2cn4

Intelligence:
http://www.bbc.co.uk/programmes/p00545l3

Jung: http://www.bbc.co.uk/programmes/p004y2bf

Language and the Mind:
http://www.bbc.co.uk/programmes/p00545cr

Memory: http://www.bbc.co.uk/programmes/p00545jl

Neuroscience:
http://www.bbc.co.uk/programmes/b00fbd26

Religion

Angels: http://www.bbc.co.uk/programmes/p003k9gf

The Apocalypse:
http://www.bbc.co.uk/programmes/p0054914

The Buddha:
http://www.bbc.co.uk/programmes/p00548br

Calvinism:
http://www.bbc.co.uk/programmes/b00qvqpz

Catharism:
http://www.bbc.co.uk/programmes/p005488v

Death: http://www.bbc.co.uk/programmes/p00546ry

The Devil:
http://www.bbc.co.uk/programmes/p005494p

The Diet of Worms:
http://www.bbc.co.uk/programmes/p0038x8z

The Fall: http://www.bbc.co.uk/programmes/p004y27p

Fundamentalism:
http://www.bbc.co.uk/programmes/p00545gy

Good and Evil:
http://www.bbc.co.uk/programmes/p00545g0

Heaven: http://www.bbc.co.uk/programmes/p003k9lf

Hell: http://www.bbc.co.uk/programmes/p0038xb6

The Jesuits:
http://www.bbc.co.uk/programmes/b007731w

Miracles: http://www.bbc.co.uk/programmes/b00dkh78

The Nicene Creed:
http://www.bbc.co.uk/programmes/b008jglt

The Schism:
http://www.bbc.co.uk/programmes/p0054921
St. Paul: http://www.bbc.co.uk/programmes/b00kjk8z

The Soul: http://www.bbc.co.uk/programmes/p00548q4

Sunni and Shia Islam:
http://www.bbc.co.uk/programmes/b00l5mhl

Zoroastrianism:
http://www.bbc.co.uk/programmes/p005bc5v

DVDs

Brian Greene   The Elegant Universe
James Burke   Connections
                        The Day The Universe Changed
History Channel   The American Revolution
                        The French Revolution
                        The Presidents
                        Rome
BBC Video   The First World War
                        Planet Earth
                        The Blue Planet
Ken Burns   The Civil War
                        Thomas Jefferson
                        The War
                        Lewis and Clark
The Learning Company   The History of Ancient Egypt
                        The New Testament
                        A History of European Art
                        Books That Have Made History

CPSIA information can be obtained at www.ICGtesting.com
Printed in the USA
BVOW08s2038210715

409755BV00002B/6/P